THE SKIER'S BIBLE

THE SKIER'S BIBLE

by Morten Lund

General Editor, SKI MAGAZINE

Junior Bounous, one of the eat American skiers and ski inuctors.

Doubleday & Company, Inc., Garden City, New York

This book is dedicated to Bill Briggs,

ski teacher extraordinary,

and to my father, who put me on skis.

PHOTO CREDITS

Foreword

Morten Lund is easily one of the two or three top writers on ski technique in this country. His editorial collaboration with the leading ski school directors over the past fifteen years in writing basic and advanced theoretical articles has given him a breadth of experience that no other writer can match. In this book, he fills a long-standing need. Too often ski books have been merely one exercise after another, without giving the skier a sense of where he is going and why. In this book the text starts right out by explaining with crystal simplicity what it is that makes a pair of straight skis able to turn. From there on the skier is shown what each step does for him in terms of his goals. The author takes the reader inside the world of teaching and tells the skier how to pick the best route for *his* individual needs.

This book ought to make both skier and ski instructor aware that there is more to ski learning than a set of standard steps. The author treats with insight the various classic and revolutionary methods at work on the American ski scene at present: his book includes the American and Canadian techniques, the Walter Foeger parallel school, learning with short skis; it includes methods used by some of the outstanding ski schools in the country. To my mind, there is no book like this one on the market today.

This book ought to make better skiers and better ski instructors. It will certainly help its reader to an understanding of all teaching in the United States, something that no other book has even attempted.

Taken together with the chapters on equipment, clothing, safety, and so on, this presentation of technique and teaching methods makes this a true *Skier's Bible*.

JUNIOR BOUNOUS

Provo, Utah
March, 1968

Contents

Preface

This book is, among other things, the first attempt to see what each of the various ski-teaching systems in the country has to offer the skier. It is written in the sure knowledge that the skiers of this country—Eastern and Western—are a different breed from their fellow skiers in the rest of the world.

The American skier plays on a higher level and plays at a faster pace. He skis better than any other country's recreational skiers, because he tries harder. And, although he's number one, he wants to get still better. He thinks in terms of skiing steeper trails, and skiing them in all conditions. He believes the key to the magic realm of the expert lies in technique.

The American instructor tries hard to oblige. He and his fellows have organized: their aim being to make skiing easier, to teach it faster.

The biggest and best-known group is the Professional Ski Instructors of America. There are also certified Canadian ski schools; there are Walter Foeger *Natur Teknik* ski schools, and there are schools that attempt to apply the insights of the Clif Taylor short-ski theory. The first chapter of the book will look into how these schools are measuring up.

The rest of the book is concerned with imparting the know-how that the author has picked up in twenty years of skiing. This includes advice on terrain, equipment, etiquette, safety, competitive skiing, and ski areas in various parts of the United States and Canada.

Read on for good skiing!

MORTEN LUND

Chapter 1

MODERN SKIING

What modern skiing is and how it looks; how to learn it

It is with some hesitation that I use the word "modern" in this chapter heading. Every system that has come into the world in recent centuries has been labeled *modern*. However, I shall try to place the word in perspective, running a small detour first.

The most valuable asset a skier can have in learning to ski, once he is off the slope, is a book of good ski-sequence pictures. They help to train the eye, and a good eye for ski form in important.

The choice of a demonstrator for ski-sequence photographs is important also, and I was fortunate in obtaining the cooperation of Don Pearsons of the Killington, Vermont, ski school, and of Karl Pfeiffer, head of the ski school. Pfeiffer is a truly compassionate ski-school director, and his school is a most progressive element on the ski-teaching scene today.

The best form in which to accomplish almost any turn is called "parallel." In parallel skiing, the skier keeps his skis pretty much together and pointed in the same direction at all times. Teaching today is directed toward this goal.

2. *Don Pearsons.*

3. *Karl Pfeiffer.*

4.   *Hannes Schneider, founder of the Arlberg School of ski teaching, the first success-ful method in the history of the sport.*

5. *Touring in old-fashioned equipment of the Hannes Schneider era.*

Little wonder. Parallel skiing is a thing of beauty: the skier flows down the slope with a motion that is near kin to ballet. To master parallel is a joy in itself. The first and second chapters of this book deal with this goal: the parallel turn.

The third and fourth chapters are devoted to the modern "short" parallel turn. This means largely "wedel," that ultimate of parallel technique, a way of skiing that stands near the peak of achievement.

Subsequent chapters set down the practical steps by which a skier can extract the best

from each of several different ski-teaching systems.

The ski techniques we see today have grown from a double root. One is the "stem" root, which began when Hannes Schneider developed a method for teaching Austrian soldiers how to ski. The early Schneider school flourished in the Arlberg region of the Austrian peaks. The Arlberg system is the "stem technique."

The other root is the "parallel" root, which began with another Austrian, Toni Seelos. Herr Seelos was primarily a racer and a coach rather than an instructor. For many years, Schneider

6

7

was the giant and Seelos the underdog. Schneider dominated the early ski-teaching business. He came at a time when there were many conflicting techniques; he cleared them out in favor of the Arlberg. The Schneider school was strong because it was the first teaching method to incorporate a learning "ladder," systematic steps which led to technical perfection. It was the first true "system" or "method."

8

9. *Using the snowplow to control a downhill course: the skier is making a series of snowplow turns down a mountain.*

THE ARLBERG TECHNIQUE

The Arlberg technique itself was designed for utility. It could carry a soldier down a hill steadily and slowly. It allowed the civilian to hike miles to a mountain on skis in a loose "touring" binding (all that skiers had available then). The solid, steady, and precise characteristics of the Arlberg all depended on the use of "the stem."

A stem, quite simply, is a position in which the skier holds the skis with the tips together and the tails apart, so that he resembled a man riding a snowplow. (Picture 6.) In fact, the stem and the "snowplow" are identical positions, but the terms designate different kinds of turns in the same position (we'll go into the difference later).

If we watch a skier in "running position" (Picture 7), we see that he is going downhill and will accelerate to higher and higher speeds unless something is done about it. One solution is a stem or a snowplow. Any skier can slow down considerably just by adopting this position.

Schneider proposed that the skier do just that: go into the stem whenever he felt he was going too fast. A proficient snowplow or stem skier can go down almost any mountain from top to bottom in a fairly straight line at slow speed, for the snowplow and stem act as brakes.

More than that, the snowplow or stem can be used as a steering device.

How do the snowplow and stem actually turn a skier? The answer is simple; also it shows why some positions will and others will not turn the skier.

S AND G FORCES

When a skier steps into place on a ski and stands normally, his center of gravity will be just to the rear of the center of the ski. (Picture 8.) All bindings are set accordingly. If we call the skier's weight "G," we can see that G is pressing down just behind the center.

When a skier is in the snowplow, each ski has a force of gravity pulling it from that point where the weight of the skier lies upon each ski. (Picture 9.) Essentially it means that we

G and S pushing at different points tend to spin the ski

have G1, the weight on one ski, and G2, the weight on the other ski, both wanting to pull the skis straight down the hill. If there were no other forces involved, there would be no possibility of turning. The skier would have to go straight down the hill. If the skier were on a sheet of steel instead of snow, this would be the situation indeed.

But snow makes a difference. It provides a second force working on the skis. This is the *resistance* of the snow. This second force we can call S1 and S2. It pushes up the hill against the skis. It pushes at a point we can call the "center of resistance," which is just ahead of the middle of the ski. (Picture 10.) In other words, S pushes up just in front of the point at which G pulls down. (Picture 11.)

G pulls downward just *behind* the center of the ski.

S pushes upward just *ahead* of the center of the ski.

As you come down a hill in the plow position, the skis will want to turn, but each wants to turn the skier in a different direction. As you look at the picture, G1 and S1 are trying to spin one ski, at the left, in a counterclockwise direction, and G2 and S2 are trying to spin the other ski, at your right, in a clockwise direction. As long as both skis are trying equally hard to spin, it will be a standoff. The skier will not turn either way. He'll go straight down, with both skis trying to spin but not able to. All that will happen is that the skier will slow down. But if one ski could get a stronger spin than

skier leans on one ski

13

skier leans on the other ski

14

the other, this ski would win out and would spin in the direction it wanted and the skier with it. He would go down the slope in a slow spin. *This is a turn.* (Picture 13.)

In order to turn, the skier merely puts more

weight on one ski. Putting more weight on one ski increases the ski's tendency to spin. This ski wins out. Leaning on the right ski, as in Picture 13, causes that ski to spin the skier counterclockwise. Leaning on the left ski, as in

15

16

skier lifts entire
ski off

17

skier lifts
tails off

18

Picture 14, causes this ski to turn the skier clockwise. The act of leaning is called "weight shift."

A skier can make one snowplow turn after another simply by shifting his weight first to the one ski and then to the other. He will turn first to the left and then to the right.

THE PARALLEL TURN

But, while turning in a stem or snowplow is fun, there is a more elegant way to turn, the way discovered by Seelos not too long after Hannes Schneider had settled on his stem technique.

Take a skier going straight down the hill. (Picture 15.) In running position, his skis are pretty much together. Gravity (G) pulls him straight down the line of his skis. But if he can somehow pick both skis up a bit and land them, still parallel, at an angle to the original path of the skis, snow resistance (S) will become strong. Both skis will go into a spin in the same direction because of the S and G

forces. (Picture 16.) This is much more powerful and efficient than a stem turn. In a stem, the skis always fight each other to some extent, even though one wins out. In a parallel turn, with both skis together, the skis are helping each other.

Snow forces push the front of the skis upward and gravity pulls the tails down, just so long as the skis skid sidewise a bit.

The parallel turn is made with S and G forces, but the turn is smooth and sophisticated: the skier balances over two skis together, rather than over two skis inelegantly far apart as in the stem or snowplow position. The parallel turn is a graceful swoop compared to the dogged look of the plow.

Because it looks good and because it works so well, parallel has been a desirable technique ever since Seelos first mastered it as a racing technique; it has been the ideal of skiers for racing and recreation.

Almost all modern ski learning revolves around two key points. The first is to get the beginning skier most quickly to the stage where he can make the skidding, swooping parallel turn. This

19. *The old-fashioned rotation method of turning. The skiers have "unweighted" and "blocked" the forward turn of arm and upper body. As a result, the skis have skidded into the beginning of a parallel turn.*

20

is called "method" or "teaching method." The second big consideration is how to achieve that important movement of the skis out of their path to *begin* the skid that starts a parallel turn. This is called "technique" or "parallel technique." There are different methods and different techniques.

Let's consider technique for a minute.

The skis need to be lifted a bit to get them out of the "groove" or "track" they have been running in, first, in order to *turn* them at an angle to the groove so they'll start skidding. This "lift" can be provided by a short upward hop. Skiers call this hop "up-motion"; the result is "unweighting." (The skis go weightless for a second.) A quick hop can lift the whole ski off the snow. (Picture 17.)

A more sophisticated way to do it is to hop the tails off only, keeping the tips in contact with the snow. (Picture 18.)

Once the skier is in the air in this "unweighted" position, he has to *turn* the skis. This calls for the exerting of some sort of muscle power *after* the hop. Gravity and the snow are not going to turn the skis for the skier, initially, in a parallel turn.

ROTATION AND REVERSE PARALLEL

In the early days of skiing, starting with See-los, the "turning force" in the unweighted position was called "rotation."

To use rotation to turn the skis, the skier had to wind up first while he was still on the snow. That means he'd pull his outside arm and shoulder back. ("Outside" refers to the outside of the turn.) Then, before he started the hop, he'd swing this outside arm and shoulder forward by "rotating" his upper body from the waist up. (Picture 19.) Then he would hop and at the same time stop or "block" this rotation motion as he hopped. This caused the turning movement of the upper body to go to the lower body as well. The whole body therefore turned a bit, and the skis with it. The skier came down again on the snow with the skis turned or "displaced," and from there the S and G forces on the skis would finish it for the skier, letting him arc around in a wide turn.

This was rotation.

21

22

24

23

The trouble is that, for a beginning skier, rotation is a rather difficult, three-part kind of motion: windup, blocking, and turning. Not many skiers did it with ease. As a result, beginners did not learn parallel skiing very fast if at all. They tended to use stem skiing to start with and never got to parallel.

This was the situation in 1950, when a new phenomenon, a new kind of turning power, began to replace rotation.

The new force was called "reverse."

Suppose you are standing on a small rug on a highly polished bare wood floor. If you want to turn your toes in an entirely new direction quickly, you would instinctively use "reverse turning power."

Try it. You will notice that in turning the feet around so that the toes point in another direction, the shoulder twists slightly in the direction *opposite* the foot turn. (Picture 20.) In other words, you will end up facing slightly farther left in order to make the toes point farther right.

The "reverse" action of the upper body provides a kind of leverage for the lower body so that it can turn quickly and forcefully.

The explanation of the effect is this: the muscles of the mid-body are the ones that twist the lower body (and the feet with it) in a new direction. But these midsection muscles are fastened to the upper *and* lower body. To twist the lower body one way, they have to twist the upper body in the other, automatically.

Suppose a skier wants to make a reverse parallel turn. He goes down the slope; he hops up (unweights). (Pictures 21 and 22.) Then, without any preliminary windup, he uses the mid-body muscles to twist the skis so that they turn in a new direction (more to the reader's left). The same muscles in the same move turn the upper body in the opposite direction (to the reader's right). (Picture 23.) When he comes down, the skis will be turned so that the S and G forces will take over. Then S and G obligingly finish off the turn for him. (Pictures 23 and 24.)

What is so good about the "reverse"?

The reverse turn needs no preparatory windup. You can do it instantly. You can do many turns in rapid sequence, and this is impossible with the rotation turn. Much of modern skiing on slopes (and particularly slalom racing) demands fast and shorter turns for safety and control. It was inevitable that the reverse-powered turn should replace rotation, as it has to a great extent.

There are still times when it is convenient, and fun, besides, to turn with rotation. Seelos' work was not all in vain. *The* modern turn, however, is the reverse turn.

The other big question, how to bring the beginning skier most quickly to the parallel turn is still in the process of being settled.

So, let's consider "method," or the way in which we attain parallel skiing.

The ideal system, obviously, would be to have the skier *start* on parallel turns, even rough parallel turns, so that he would never have to make a stem. Once you "ski stem," it's a real habit. Also, parallel turns have a lot more fun and grace to them, and a swinging feel. The skier who could do parallel from the beginning would have more fun. He would learn faster.

But alas, the steps that compose the parallel turn are fairly sophisticated: there is the hop, the turning of the skis, the controlled sidewise and forward slide with the S and G forces working for you. All this requires balance and feel for the skis.

Ski teachers persisted, however, in developing more elegant and efficient teaching methods. Finally, one school (Walter Foeger's *Natur Teknik*) confidently advertised that it could teach the average skier parallel from the first day on. Another school uses a short-ski technique that makes it quite easy for skiers to make parallel turns from the beginning. Other schools found out how to put students through the stem phases and onto the parallel much more quickly than before.

In the next chapters we're going to examine the methods of teaching, so that you can get the best out of each method for yourself.

Chapter 2

SPEED CONTROL

What the turn does for you; one example of a system that builds the skier up to a parallel turn; skiing terms

When we consider the parallel turn, we must realize that its most important function is to act as a brake.

To understand this, consider a skier coming down the hill in running position. If he is coming straight down, he is running "in the fall line." (Picture 25.)

The fall line is an important idea in skiing: it is a line that you always refer to in thinking about your turns. The fall line can be defined as the path a falling object would take down the hill from any point on the hill. For any given skier, the fall line runs straight down the hill from him.

shallow traverse

27

Any path other than the fall line is called a "traverse."

A traverse, obviously, is a slower path down the hill than the fall line. But in the case of a steep traverse, as in Picture 26, it is not much slower.

Fortunately, there are also "shallow traverses," which are fairly slow paths. (Picture 27.)

One result of a turn is to get the skier into a shallow traverse. This traverse slows the skier down considerably. If he really wants to, he can even go from a shallow traverse to run up the hill for a bit; then he'll soon stop. (Picture 28.) Obviously, then, a turn can slow a skier down by putting him on a shallow traverse. But this is only one way a turn slows you down.

The second slowdown factor is the drag effect of "sideslipping."

A ski that is turning, obviously, is not going straight down the hill. To some extent it is skidding sideways down the hill (it is also moving forward). In the stem, for instance, the skier

horizontal traverse

28

29. *The skid effect of a turn is shown here. The skier throws snow to the outside of the turn, because the skis skid sideways as well as moving forward in the turn. Notice the flow of the snow out from under the tips to the outside, toward the reader.*

holds the skis out to the side so that they skid sideways. In the parallel, the skier uses his speed to hop the skis and skid the skis sideways.

The sideways progress, called "sideslip" or "skid," always takes place when a ski is turning. A ski can't turn without some sideslip.

The spray of snow that the skis of a fast skier throws to the outside of a turn is a result of the braking effect (Picture 29) of sideslip.

The turns that skiers make when they weave a snake trail down a slope are not made just for fun (although they are fun, too); the skids or sideslips have a *braking* effect, slowing the skier down and keeping him in control. The steeper the hill the more turns are needed.

The reason that a beginner is confined to

moderate slopes is that a snowplow turn takes a while to execute; he would be going forty miles an hour if he were on a steep slope.

Parallel turns, on the other hand, can be executed much more quickly. The sooner the skier learns parallel, the sooner he is going to be able to have fun on the steeper slopes. The progressive ski schools in the country are bending every effort to getting skiers to parallel quickly.

THE FOEGER SYSTEM

To get a rough idea of how a ski school brings the skier along, let's take a quick look at the *Natur Teknik* school, founded by Walter Foeger, recently retired. Foeger's method is a bit simpler to grasp than the standard methods used by the schools run by teachers of the Professional Ski Instructors of America (PSIA).

The Foeger school teaches "direct parallel."

I use this term to contrast his method with that of the Austrian and PSIA schools, which teach the plow first, then the stem, and finally, through various other steps, the parallel.

Like the PSIA's American method, the Foeger system used the reverse-powered start for the turns. Foeger is much more forceful in introducing the reverse motion, however. He teaches the motion at the start, giving the skier a chance to practice coordinating various parts of the reverse motion long before he actually uses it. Foeger's method has been called a "hop" method. This description is an oversimplification, but Foeger does give the hop an important role. The skier, in one of his first exercises, stands in place and hops the tails of the skis off the snow. (Picture 30.) He subsequently hops the tails to one side.

We pause here for a moment to note that the skier who hops the ski tails left, for instance, is doing approximately the same thing as a skier who swings the tips of his skis to the right. Both actions are right turns, in effect, and will serve to start the skis to complete an arc, the arc being finished off by S and G forces. As you can see by comparing Picture 31 with Picture 30, the skier who swings the tips left will have started just about the same kind of turn as a skier who hops the tails right. The

30   31

32

original ski positions

new ski position

33

34

35

sideslip with turning

36

sideslip without turning

37

hop takes a bit more energy, because it moves the whole skier. The skier who swings his tips is merely twisting his feet in place.

In the Foeger hop, the skier learns to hop the tails of the skis to one side, and simultaneously to turn the upper body to face that side. The skier stands with his ski tips at a certain point on a flat area (Picture 32), hops the tails to one side, faces that side, and lands with the tips still at point (1). (Picture 33.)

This quarter-turn of the upper body counterclockwise is really a reverse movement, since it is coupled with what is essentially a turn of the skis clockwise. Body right, tips left. This is the reverse.

Or, to put it the way it is taught, "Hop tails left, face left." This is reverse.

Now, after he has gotten the reverse-movement idea, the Foeger skier goes on to learn how to use snow and gravity to finish off the turn. This part of the teaching starts out with the sideslip or, as Foeger preferred to call it, "side slide."

The sideslip or side slide is a skid achieved without any turning of the ski. It is a preparation for letting the ski turn as it skids.

Any skier standing with skis pointed across the face of the hill can keep them there simply by "edging." He forces the upper edge of each ski into the snow by pressing his knees in toward the hill and, leaning out over the skis to maintain his balance; he puts most of the weight on the downhill or lower ski. (Picture 34.) He will *not* slide sidewise downhill.

But if he now *flattens* the skis so that they lie against the slant of the hill, the skis will move sideways down the hill, slowly. (Picture 35.) This is sideslip or side slide.

SIDE SLIDE

In doing the side slide, the skier has to lean forward to such an extent that his weight will put the pull of gravity, G, exactly opposite the snow-force push, S. Otherwise S and G will act at different points and turn the skis as the skier slides down. (Picture 36.) When the skier moves his weight so that it acts at the same point as S, then S and G neutralize each other and there is no turning of the skis. (Picture 37.) In Picture 36, the skier's weight is back, and the skis are turning as he slides down. In Picture 37, the skier has moved his weight a bit forward, and the skis slide down in a nice side slide *without* any turning of the skis up the hill.

38

straight
original path

tails
move
downhill

new
curving path

39

G

S

40

Next the Foeger skier does his first real turn, using the reverse motion to start it, and the S and G forces to finish the turn. This simple parallel turn is called the "uphill christie."

In the advanced form of the uphill christie, the skier runs along a traverse. (Picture 38.) He edges his skis so that they cannot slide sideways. But when he flattens his skis, the G force working from the side starts turning the skis. (Picture 39.) The reason it turns the skis is that he is standing straight over his bindings, and, as in Picture 36, this makes the skis turn while they are skidding because S and G are working at different points on the ski. (If he leaned forward, they would skid without turning, as in Picture 37.)

The skier is now moving forward, his skis are sideslipping, and they are turning away from the valley, toward the hill. (This is why it is called the *uphill* christie.) When the skis turn far enough, the skier will be running in a shallow traverse and will be slowed down. (Picture 40.)

Many skiers use the simple uphill christie to end their turn and come to a halt.

This turn is not quite so simple as it seems, however. The flattening of the skis is a fairly subtle process. The beginning skier is not used to exerting this fine an edge control. That is, he is not used to holding the raised edges of the skis precisely an inch less or an inch more toward or away from the snow. Making a ski lie "flatter" or "more on edge" is hard to accom-

41

42

43

plish until the skier has practiced it many times.

In the Foeger system, therefore, and in the American system too, the skier first goes into a crouch. (Picture 41.) Then he hops, (Picture 42.) Then he uses the reverse motion to turn the skis. (Picture 43.) The minute the skis are turned off the track by the skier's reverse motion, of course, some skidding takes place, and the S and G forces go to work turning the ski.

This "crouch, hop, and reverse" is a way of forcing the uphill christie to happen. And it does happen, even if the skier's edge control is a bit ragged. This hop is called up-unweighting.

Incidentally, Foeger called the uphill christie "turn to the mountain." This term means that

the tips of the skis are swinging toward the mountain peak rather than toward the valley.

The Foeger skier who has reached the point where he can make the turn up the hill from a shallow traverse is now on the way to making a parallel turn of a more demanding sort.

He first makes his uphill christie from a somewhat steeper traverse, and then from a still steeper traverse (all on a moderate slope). Finally, he makes the turn from the fall line.

This means that, having started a run down the fall line and having gone for a distance, he crouches and hops and makes his reverse. There follows a long turning slide as the S and G forces take over to finish the turn. (Picture 44.)

This uphill christie from the fall line is also called a "christie from the fall line."

Also, it can be described as "the last half of a full parallel turn."

THE FULL PARALLEL TURN

What is a full parallel turn?

The christie from the fall line starts with the tips turning up the hill while the full parallel turn starts with the tips "down the hill," and *then* ends with a turn up the hill. Thus, the parallel turn can be thought of as having these two parts (Picture 45): the first part, in which

shoulders turn left

up motion

ski tails turn toward right

44

the skier turns the tips from the traverse down the hill into the fall line (Positions A through C), and the second, where the skier turns the tips out of the fall line up the hill back to the new traverse. (Positions C to E.)

This latter part is nothing but a "christie from the fall line."

Obviously, it is easier to learn this second part. Here, the skier is continuously slowing down as he comes out of the fall line, because

he is headed for a shallow traverse. (In the first part of the turn, going steeper and steeper into the fall line, he is speeding up.)

Foeger called the first part of the parallel turn "the turn downhill." Obviously, when the skier starts trying this part of the turn, he'd better know the following part by heart, so that he can pull out of the turn easily and quickly and come to a gradual slowdown.

The Foeger skier prepares for this "turn down-

first traverse

fall line

A

B

C

skis
turn
downhill

D

E

new traverse

47

46

48

hill" by doing further reverse-motion exercises at a standstill, on the flat. He is going to start the full parallel turn with reverse motion, and so he needs the practice. Once he starts the turn, however, the S and G forces will take him into the fall line and out again in the uphill christie, to safety.

This needs a bit of diagraming.

49

In the first part of the parallel turn, we can say that the G force includes the force of the skier's speed along the traverse, a speed built up by gravity.

The force built up by the skier's speed along the traverse path will tend to make him continue that path. (Picture 46.) When the skis are twisted or hopped out of that path (with or without the help of the ski pole) and start out in a new direction, the G force then will push the tails of the skis toward the outside of the turn. Since the ski is skidding a bit, the S force comes along to push the tips toward the center of the turn. (Picture 47.)

The skier can finish off the parallel turn simply by holding his position: this is a question of balancing over the outside ski and letting the S and G forces do the rest of the work. (Pictures 47 to 49.)

This turn is the goal of the Foeger skier.

This same parallel is also the goal of the American system, but the American-system skier gets it more gradually, going through stem turns first.

There are advantages to both ways of getting to parallel, and we'll discuss these in later chapters.

POLE HANDLING

Since we have mentioned poles for the first time, it should be said that, in the modern theory of recreational skiing, you should be able to do all turns on moderate terrain without the use of poles. Poles are really necessary on steep terrain only.

The function of the pole is to help the skier hop or rise in the unweighting movement. The pole should be placed in the snow pointing pretty much in the same direction as the skis. If you plant the pole so that the tip points in toward the skis, then the chances are that you are trying to "hook" yourself into the turn, instead of using reverse or rotation to start you into the turn.

Most beginners tend to put their hand through the loop of the pole strap and then grasp only the pole. This is wrong. Pictures 50 and 51

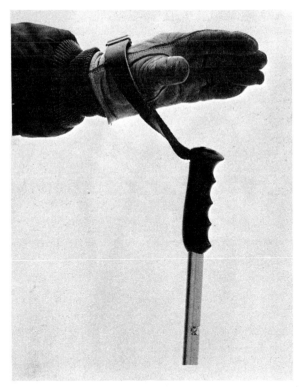

50

51

show that the hand is put through the loop and then *both* the loop and the pole are grasped. This positions your hand properly on the pole handle. When using the pole, let the strap take the strain. You don't need to clench the pole hard. In fact, if you use the strap properly, you can leave your hand partly open and relaxed, as in Picture 51, as you use the pole.

The ultimate goal of both Foeger and American systems is the same: the full parallel turn, starting in one traverse and finishing in the traverse going in the opposite direction. There is no fundamental disagreement.

What we have, rather, is an exact illustration of the difference between "method" and "technique." Paul Valar, the ski school director at Cannon Mountain, New Hampshire, has headed the long effort of PSIA to establish an American system. One of Valar's really valuable contributions to the ski world was to insist on this distinction. Technique is the polished movements of the accomplished skier. Method is how he is taught these movements.

Obviously, a reverse-turn skier would look different to a marked degree from a rotation skier on the slope, and so we would say that these *techniques* are different. Yet a fully trained Foeger skier and a fully turned-out American-system skier would look pretty much the same, given minor latitude in arm positions and other details. Both make reverse parallel turns. Thus, we say that here the *technique* is the same, but the *method* of reaching it is different.

We have gotten a good way from our starting point, which was speed control. And yet, we have stayed on the subject. Speed control means the parallel turn, if we are looking for the ultimate. And the Foeger system, which we have viewed briefly (we shall come back to it again), is solely concerned with the parallel turn; we can now see what makes up a parallel turn.

The second purpose of this chapter is to give you an idea of how a ski system puts together a ladder of progress toward a turn. It is not just a question of having the skier get out there and try to make a full parallel turn. He can do the easy parts first.

Lastly, the third function of this chapter has been to give you an idea of what some of the basic skiing terms are.

Just so that you don't forget them, let's review a few terms we have run across in the previous pages.

turn—any curved path on the slopes made by the skis.

fall line—the steepest way down the hill from any given point on the hill.

traverse—any straight path other than the fall line.

christie—a sliding turn, or the sliding part of any turn. (The original name comes from Christiania, the old name of Oslo, capital of Norway; the turn was invented in the neighborhood.)

uphill christie—a turn from a traverse to a shallower traverse with skis parallel. The easiest parallel turn.

turn to the mountain—same as uphill christie.

turn out of the fall line—same as uphill christie, but starting in the fall line.

edge control—the ability to flatten the skis or put them on edge as required by circumstances.

method—the way in which technique is acquired.

technique—the final look of the skier, including the kinds of turning power that he employs, the latter being the main factor dividing one technique from another.

turn into the fall line—a turn that goes from a traverse into the fall line.

turn downhill—same as turn into the fall line.

full turn—a turn from a traverse into the fall line and then out of the fall line again, to a traverse.

direct parallel—a method of teaching parallel from the beginning of a skier's lessons.

sideslipping—going sideways downhill by flattening the skis against the hill until they start sliding sideways.

side-sliding—same as sideslipping.

Chapter 3

MAKING MANY TURNS

The necessity for quick turns in succession;
how ski length affects the quickness of
the turn

52. *Clif Taylor, inventor of the short ski, does a quick jump in his shortest version, the two-and-a-half-foot ski.*

This chapter will take up the idea broached in the last one: the idea of making many quick turns to get the maximum in speed control.

Even with parallel turns, there is difficulty in making them short enough to get really good control. When you watch a well-trained skier come down an expert slope, you see him bobbing in a continuous up-and-down rhythm, a succession of hops, one hop to each turn. He keeps the skis' speed down by these turns, and it is a beautiful piece of work to watch.

If only beginners could get something approximating this kind of control, they would be better off right from the start. Short turns equal safety.

But the coordination needed to coordinate the hops and the reverse motions with the pole work for short turns is obviously quite beyond the skill of even the best of beginners.

The only way would be to make the skis "easier" somehow. And this is the way one solution actually came about.

The solution came through Clif Taylor, an instructor in the ski school at Hogback Mountain in Brattleboro, Vermont. Taylor had some pupils who were experimenting on their own in the use of shorter skis. They simply sawed off the tails of old pairs of long skis. Taylor became intrigued, because it seemed to help their skiing, and he designed a pair of five-foot skis (normal skis run six feet or longer) for his pupils. They worked better than sawed-off skis. Taylor's pupils were happy, and they skied better than ever.

Taylor now began to think about ski lengths in earnest. He wondered how short you could

counter-clockwise motion of upper body and arms

clockwise motion of lower body and skis

53

nique added to short skis brought about a potential revolution in the treatment of the beginning skier.

The first step of the Taylor *method* is to have the skier swing the skis back and forth on the flat while standing in place. The lower body swings with the skis, and the upper body swings in the opposite direction, so that we get a series of quick, reverse-powered turns in place. (Picture 53.)

This same twist is next done while the skier moves down the hill (Picture 54), making a series of short, connected turns. The skier does most of the turning with his mid-body muscle. The turns are so short there is very little time for the S and G forces to act. The Taylor method makes the kickoff of the turn, the reverse-power movement, all-important. There is so little friction under the short ski that the skier doesn't have to work with S and G forces by balancing exactly over the skis. This simplifies things tremendously. And, again, he doesn't have to hop to start the skis going. Even

make a ski and still have something skiable. He experimented with four-foot designs and then with even shorter ones. He got down to a two-and-a-half-foot design, which would just hold a boot and a binding. He obtained good results with the four-footers and the two-footers in his beginning classes. Almost anyone could start skiing on the two-footers without much strain, he found.

THE TWIST METHOD

After a bit of experimenting, Taylor also found that, by using a "twist" turning process, he could get people to make short, connected parallel turns the *first* day they got on skis. The beauty of it, Taylor found, was that the two-footers needed no "hop" to start them turning. They could be twisted into the turn with a reverse motion. Taylor had essentially reduced the problem of turning parallel skis by reducing the size of the skis. The "twist" teaching tech-

traversing

turning

54

though the Taylor twist exercise in Picture 53 is related to the Foeger "hop and twist," Taylor's exercise is much easier and less acrobatic.

What can the beginning skier get out of the Taylor system?

In the first place, he can go up the ski lift within a few hours of getting on the skis. By contrast, the American-system skiers and the Foeger-system skiers will have to wait more than half a day, at minimum, and more likely as much as two days, before they get their long skis sufficiently under control to go up a ski lift. The users of the short ski have more fun.

The skier on short skis gets tremendous *motivation*. He can make a *series* of parallel turns. He is *able* to make turns right away, and these are the parallel turns he wants to perfect. He doesn't have to detour into different *kinds* of turns along the way. This is advantage number two.

One of the hardest things for beginning skiers to do is to connect their turns, one after the other. And yet closely connected turns mean safety and control. The rhythm that can be worked up on the short skis is exactly the same reverse-powered rhythm (with the bobbing left out) that must be achieved on long skis if one is to do well on steeper slopes.

Third advantage: he is making *short* turns.

He is not likely to learn short turns to begin with by any other method in most ski schools. Although I cannot quite fathom why, the ski schools—American, Foeger, and Canadian—seem unanimous in urging the *long* parallel turn upon the pupil early in parallel skiing, before he has mastered a *short* parallel turn. Since it is the short parallel that gives the skier the best control, and since it is essentially easier than the long parallel (I shall elaborate on this later), the effort to teach long parallel turns first is in the wrong direction.

Fourth advantage: the skier can progress by stages, using short, controlled turns all the time—two-and-a-half-foot ski, four-foot ski, five-foot ski, to as long a ski as the skier can handle. By these stages he can achieve parallel, long turn and all, as well as wedel on the long ski.

A good number of schools, particularly Karl Pfeiffer's school at Killington, Vermont, have adopted short skis as a more effective method of teaching skiers; they gradually increase the length of the skis each day or two in class. This is called "Graduated Length Method," or GLM.

Fifth: the skier can find out what is the best length of ski for him.

SKI LENGTH

The traditional answer to proper ski length, the one that most skiers and ski-shop salesman will give you, is that the proper length of ski for the beginning skier is the length from the heel of the skier's upraised palm down to the floor, assuming the skier is holding his hand straight up overhead as high as he can hold it.

This is not necessarily the proper length of ski for just any skier unfortunately. But it is, as any racer will tell you, the proper length for a racing ski. Most shops are selling skiers a racing-length ski, which is about as sensible as selling an "Indianapolis 500" racing car to a housewife.

Fortunately, the palm-to-floor-length rule is slowly giving way, mostly under the impact of the short-ski idea. Many instructors have told me that, as a rule of thumb, they prefer to see the *average* skier with skis a foot shorter than racing length. And they like to see a *beginner* with skis no taller than himself.

If such skiers continue skiing and improve, they might want to get longer skis, of course. But some skiers who *start* with the long racing ski find it so difficult that they often give up the sport right away—in spite of good instruction and good intentions.

The real test of the proper length is not a rule of thumb, but the longest ski you can handle on the slopes you intend to ski.

Taylor's phrase for it is "I'd rather have the challenge in the mountain than in the skis."

Why go on to long skis at all if the short skis are so easy?

There are a number of answers. The first is pride in having skis as long as everybody else.

55. *The old-fashioned hanging-in-the-straps kind of turn, no longer much used today.*

There is nothing wrong with legitimate pride.

A more practical reason is this: The longer ski is like a longer wheelbase in a car. It gives a smoother ride. The long ski goes over bumps more easily, it goes through abrupt holes in better fashion, and it is generally easier-riding at high speeds.

Another practical reason is that the long ski has more speed. You may not want more speed way up on the mountain, but it is nice to have speed on the long, flat runouts at the bottom of the mountain.

A third practicality concerns soft snow. The shorter skis tend to sink, or nose in, unless the skier sits way back on the skis. The long ski will not need so much change of balance except in deep powder, in which case you have to sit back on the long ski as well.

However, the advantages of the long ski can be seen as incentives for the skier to improve so that he can handle longer skis, rather than incentives to get longer skis than he can handle.

Some American system ski schools have programs using five-foot skis supplied by the ski school. Almost all ski schools using this method report that skiers do better on five-foot skis.

There is another practical problem: there are quite a few ski schools that do not take pupils on two-and-a-half- or four-foot skis. I think that these schools are mistaken in their attitude, but it is a fact of life that many such schools do exist. They won't take skiers who show up in

56   **57**

snowplow or stem class with skis shorter than five feet.

However, if you have decided to teach *yourself* the stem and snowplow, there is no reason why you can't start on four-foot skis.

PROPER STANCE

The last subject to consider in connection with short skis is the question of stance, or the proper way to stand on skis.

It used to be that skiers thrust their weight way out ahead of their boots, "hanging in the straps." But this is now passé. On an easy slope today, a good skier keeps his weight squarely over the boots with a loose, relaxed stance. (Picture 56.)

One of the most spectacular demonstrations of the inherent balance of modern skiing occurs occasionally: a good skier's heel binding releases prematurely (as sometimes happens). He can keep on making short turns—two or three, anyway—his stance being so balanced that he doesn't need the heel binding to hold him in.

The stance that the skier *has* to adopt on short skis is essentially the modern stance. (Picture 57.)

The short skis have been criticized for lacking stability. True, they don't have the fore-and-aft support of the longer skis. But if the skier is skiing right for short turns, he doesn't need the fore-and-aft stability of the longer ski.

If the skier finds that the short ski is unstable, it is because he is not standing with the weight *over the boots*, where it should be for short turns. In effect, he is forced to stand right when he uses short skis, and this is a sort of built-in benefit for beginners who use the short ski.

Chapter 4

A HISTORY OF SHORT TURNS ON LONG SKIS

How the Austrians started a revolution and how we use it today

Something as radical as the Taylor system doesn't turn up out of the void. The ground had been prepared for it.

The history of the wedel turn is less than twenty years old. In the 1950s, the official state examiner for Austria's ski instructors, Dr. Stefan Kruckenhauser, introduced a new approach to skiing. (Actually, the Kruckenhauser system was foreshadowed by a French theorist, Georges Joubert.)

The Kruckenhauser theory arrived in the United States in the form of articles in the ski press. A few years later, it was all over but the shouting. The official Austrian system was victorious through the length and breadth of the United States.

Professor Kruckenhauser arrived at his theory by analyzing movie footage of ski racers. He was fascinated by the so-called "delayed shoulder turn" racing technique; to Kruckenhauser, it foreshadowed an entirely new department in recreational skiing.

The "delayed shoulder" was a product of slalom. This is a race in which a skier makes a number of very tight turns, often one right after the other to get through a series of paired poles, or "gates." In most slalom turns, it is an advantage for the racer to get as close to one of the poles of a gate as he can. Rotation used to be the technique of most racers, but there was a limit to how quickly one turn could follow another and also a limit to how close you could get to the pole. (Picture 58.) Skiers (mostly Austrian) who started using the delayed shoulder got closer to the proper pole. The delayed shoulder consisted of holding *back* the outside shoulder of the turn rather than thrusting it *forward* as in rotation. Holding the outside shoulder back and bending at the waist (which was made easy by holding the shoulder back) allowed the skier to brush the pole. (Picture 59.)

Slalom poles are usually passed first to the right and then to the left. What was happening was this: the left shoulder was "delayed" at one gate and the right shoulder would be delayed at the next. The upper body was turned from side to side in opposite coordination with the skis, the upper body turning in a direction opposite to that of the skis each time. A little reflection convinced Kruckenhauser that the very same middle-body muscles that were turning the upper body back and forth were also *twisting* the skis *into the turns*. In other words, the skier no longer used *rotation* to start the skis into the turn but used a series of connected

58. *A skier rotating his way around a slalom pole. Note that he isn't going to be able to get his skis very close to the pole because his left shoulder is at the pole and won't allow the skier to go any closer.*

59. *A skier reversing his way around a slalom pole. Note that the "delayed" outside shoulder lets him sneak the inside shoulder past the gate even though his skis are much closer to the gate than those of the skier in Picture 58. Also, he hits the pole with his back and slides off the pole, whereas, if he hit it with his shoulder he might get hung up on the pole.*

60

"delayed shoulder" motions. Kruckenhauser changed the name of the motion to "reverse shoulder" and announced that it *had replaced rotation.*

COUNTER-ROTATION

Another name for reverse is "counter-rotation." However, even though "counter-rotation" is the PSIA's formal word for it, "reverse" has a more immediate ring of authority to it. At any rate, the terms mean the same.

It was unfortunate, however, that all the early names for the turn called attention to the shoulder-and-upper-body motion. It was the fast twist of the lower body and the *skis* into the turn that counted. It actually does no good to swing the shoulders in the reverse movement—unless the skis can respond in the opposite direction. The upper-body motion has to be made fairly rapidly or "explosively" if it is to start the skis into the turn.

Nevertheless, Kruckenhauser set up a system of teaching that gave priority to learning the upper-body reverse movement in slow motion. The idea was that the skier could learn later to do it rapidly. The Austrian system of the 1950s got skiers to adopt the reverse position as early as the snowplow turn.

The new position created a "looking downhill" appearance. The knees were bent toward the slope, there was a bend at the waist, and the outside shoulder was back. It was called "the comma," because it did look a bit like that punctuation mark. (Picture 60.)

The comma in the snowplow position was not quite as pronounced, but it was there. (Picture 61.)

It could easily be seen in the best racing skiers. (Picture 62.)

But there was a distinction here that the Austrians were not often careful to make. The difference was between the reverse *position* and the reverse *movement*.

If the reverse movement is executed slowly, it doesn't have any effect on the skis. It doesn't

61

62. *Comma position in a race. Jean Claude Killy, one of France's great all-time racers, angulates and reverses as he goes through a gate in the 1966 Stowe Nationals, forming a comma position with his body.*

original traverse

new traverse

63

"kick" the skis into a turn. It does give the skier a good position from which to edge the skis and get the weight on the outside ski, however.

So in the early phase of the Austrian technique, "reverse" is a question of position and not of movement.

Actually, the skier doesn't need any mid-body muscle turning power, either reverse or rotation, for the plow or stem turns. These turns go from beginning to end by S and G power.

About halfway through the Austrian system, Kruckenhauser introduces "heel thrust." First at this point, the Austrian skier was using reverse power actually *to turn* the skis. A heel thrust is a very short, fast, compact uphill christie. It is, in effect, a shove of the tails downhill from a traverse. As we have seen, a shove or hop of the tails is equivalent to a twist of the whole ski.

64

65

DOWN-UNWEIGHTING

The heel thrust, then, is used to turn from a traverse into a shallower traverse, just as the uphill christie is used. In Picture 63, the skier does a heel thrust by making a quick corner at point (1), thrusting the skis downhill to point (2), and makes the thrust possible by a fast reverse motion (3), and by a dropping motion (4), which takes the weight off the skies momentarily. The skis are now turning to a shallow traverse (5).

66

67

The heel thrust can be used to go from the fall line into a shallower traverse. The motion is the same—drop and reverse. (Pictures 64 and 65.)

To most people, the "drop" or "down-un-weighting" was a big innovation. It was an unweighting by a means yet unheard of. Up to that point, all unweighting had been thought of in terms of a hop or an up-motion.

Yet the theory of the down-motion unweighting is sound.

If you stand at full height and then drop your height several inches by doing a quick knee bend, the weight is momentarily taken off the feet. For a split second it is like the sudden starting down of an elevator. You are weightless, or almost so. The period of weightlessness on skis makes it possible for the skier to twist the skis or thrust the heels of the skis.

Actually, down-unweighting and the heel thrust, which did not occupy nearly as much space in the Austrian books as the "reverse," constituted the real revolution. This quick little drop and thrust, combined with edging, was what made the racers of Austria so successful. It was not so much the delayed shoulder as the quickness of the heel thrust that got them through the slalom gates so fast.

A heel thrust from the fall line is actually a short parallel turn. A sequence of short turns made with the heel thrust—first a thrust across the fall line to the left and then a thrust to the right—is the basic ingredient both of the Austrian slalom racing style and of the famous civilian version of it, the "wedel."

In the wedel, the skier makes a series of short turns back and forth across the fall line, thrusting the tails of the skis back and forth to do it. The shoulders move back and forth a bit in the opposite direction but in short turns the shoulder motion is not so noticeable. The optical illusion is that the legs thrust first out to one side and then out to the other as the body stays motionless between. In Picture 66, the skier has just make a wedel turn to the reader's left by pushing his ski tails to the right to point (1) in a heel thrust. This is immediately

followed by a heel thrust to the right to point (2), starting a left turn (Picture 67.) One follows the other without pause, giving a snake-like look to the series of turns.

This series of turns by heel thrusts to alternate sides can also be thought of as a series of "twists" as in the Taylor method. The results of twisting the skis and of heel-thrusting are the same, but skiers think about the two differently.

Here we come to the point we brought up earlier: The short parallel turn is fairly easy to

68

69

70

do, once the reverse motion (or heel thrust) has been learned.

THE CARVED, PARALLEL TURN

The mark of the real expert, as we'll see, is not the short turn, which a lot of skiers teach themselves, but the "long, carved, parallel turn." This turn starts with a reverse (or in some cases with rotation) to set the skis at an angle to the original path. This turning power lasts only a second or so. Then, since the skis are sideslipping as well as going forward, the G and S forces take over and start to turn the skis. The skier rides these G and S forces the rest of the way around the turn, using enough edging (carving) to give him a nice smooth long arc. (Pictures 68 to 70.) This is not an easy turn, because if you edge too much, or get the weight wrong in the early part of the turn, the turn will stop cold.

Even the wedel turn can be carved to some extent by the expert. Note how much edging is being applied at the end of the turns shown in Pictures 66 and 67. The carved wedel turn is a much more precise and powerful turn than the flat-ski or "slipped" wedel. Yet, a beginning skier does not have the edge control to do a *carved* wedel turn, and so he does a flat-ski wedel. This keeps him happy. If he has to learn to carve his turns from the beginning, he will be very unhappy, because edge control of the precise sort needed for carved turns takes endless practice.

THE SLIPPED TURN

The beginner's best route is the short "slipped" parallel turn with the skis somewhat apart and quite flat all the way through. This turn is what most self-taught parallel skiers use, operating on fairly hard, smooth snow. And it works.

The short slipped parallel turn is looked upon with disdain by some instructors. They say that such a turn is merely "turning the feet." Precisely.

Yet the skier who is just getting into parallel finds this turn a lifesaver. The width between the skis has the same effect as a "canted boot." It keeps the skier's weight "off the outside edge" of the skis. Catching the outside edge is what commonly trips him in a turn. And so he can get by with less precise edge control, since his wide stance already gives him a natural tendency to edge correctly.

The self-taught parallel skier confidently slews his skis back and forth and maintains pretty good control. (Picture 71.)

beginner's
flat-ski
slewed turn

71

Here we come again to the fact that where the American system and the Foeger system teach the long carved turn first, or simultaneously, Taylor skiers have the advantage of learning the flat-ski short turn first and of having potentially better control. They can go down steeper trails sooner.

It may be argued that the skier who learns via the Taylor method or who teaches himself the slewed short turn may never get to the long carved turn. This is true. On the other hand, if he doesn't learn the short flat turn, he may never learn to ski parallel at all.

The "slewed" wedel has been named *schmieren*, which is a German word meaning "to smear." Slewing is, in essence, smearing the skis back and forth. It works pretty well as a way of controlling speed on hard-packed, fairly smooth snow, and this is the condition of the snow on which most skiers ski today anyway.

Every skier *should* eventually learn the long carved turn. There is nothing so graceful. Stein Eriksen, head of the ski school at Snowmass, Colorado, is the master of this kind of turn. He has made it his trademark. (Other components of his fame are the world championship that he won and his ability to do a full lay-out front flip on skis through the air.) The extreme long carved turn with lots of reverse and angulation is called "the Stein turn."

To summarize this chapter:

The twist and the heel thrust are sisters under the skin. The Kruckenhauser heel thrust was a way to make the long ski turn rapidly, almost in its own length, by means of a good hard reverse and a "drop," or down-unweighting. Taylor carried this to the extreme with his short skis, enabling the average beginning skier to do the same, via the twist, but without any drop-unweighting at all. The self-taught parallel skier senses that the short heel-thrust turn is the thing for him, and he manages to approximate it very aptly with a "schmieren."

We now have a good idea of what goes into parallel turns, whether short or long. Next we will take a look at the ski-teaching methods and see how these can build the skier up to the long and short parallels by a series of "teaching sequences."

Another purpose of this chapter is to set forth more ski terms. Before we go on, let's review:

carved turn—a turn with the skis edged quite sharply through the latter part of the turn.

slipped turn—a turn with the skis flat through the greater part of the turn.

down-unweighting—taking the weight off the skis with a sudden drop in the skier's height.

up-unweighting—taking the weight off the skis with a hop. (In the final form, the motion is a hop but the skis stay on the snow. This is called "up-motion.")

reverse shoulder—the drawing back of the outside shoulder of the turn, and the advancing of the inside shoulder. Used to be called "delayed shoulder."

heel thrust—a fast compact uphill christie, done with a powerful reverse motion. When done from the fall line, to either side alternately, it is like the Taylor "twist," except that it has more edging to it and is, for all practical purposes, the famous Austrian "wedel."

schmieren—the flat-ski wedel or short parallel turn typical of the self-taught skier and the Taylor short-ski system for beginners.

Chapter 5

SHORT-SKI DIRECT

Direct turning in the ski world and how it is done in the short-ski system

Hannes Schneider's sequence was a primitive one, compared to the smooth series of sequences that the ski schools build from one major step to the next in skiing today. And today there are many more sequences. These are the so-called *bridging* sequences and are at the heart of any system, whether Austrian, Foeger, French, American, Canadian, or Taylor. The skier who wants to teach himself or who wants to learn intelligently in a ski school will be 100 per cent ahead if he can grasp the gist of the sequence he is in, because sequence is the key. A good sequence is a series of exercises that brings a skier smoothly from one major stage to the next—from snowplow to stem, for instance. A bad sequence leaves the skier stranded halfway.

In Hannes' day, before the present sophistication, the skier was first put in the snowplow position and drilled until, by dint of repetition, he could do the snowplow. Then he was put into the stem position, and drilled in that. There were enough skiers who had the time and patience to undergo the drill to fill up a few ski schools in Austria. But when this system was tried upon tens of thousands of skiers in the United States, a country where the average skier did not have the time or the patience to undergo the almost military indoctrination of the Arlberg system, the dropout rate was spectacular.

The United States ski schools, therefore, have been strongly motivated to find faster ways of getting progress out of their pupils with less drill. A set of good sequences, a series of teaching aids that brings the skier from one major step to the next with minimum strain, can accomplish this. Successful sequences are like gold in the bank for any ski school that has developed them. Junior Bounous, first at Alta, Utah, then at Sugar Bowl, California, has produced sequences that he has constantly been refining, sequences that have been published to some extent by *Ski Magazine* and that have evoked widespread admiration. "Good sequences are the reason for a ski school's repeat business," said Bounous. (In his work at Sugar Bowl, Bounous was helped in developing and organizing the sequences by Bill Briggs, a particular friend of mine and a canny ski instructor who now heads the ski school at Storm King, Jackson, Wyoming.) Bounous is, incidentally, one of the best all-around skiers this country has produced. He can ski anything, because he pays attention to detail.

THE TAYLOR SYSTEM

We'll start with the bridging sequences in the Taylor system, because they are the simplest to understand in relation to the system itself.

72. *Junior Bounous, who has headed ski schools in California and Utah. His "sequences" have been widely copied in the country's ski schools.*

In the first place, we must remember that the individual major steps in the Taylor system are all full turns, right from the beginning, unlike the first steps in other systems. Therefore, the first turns in the Taylor system will tend to be executed more roughly by the learning skier. But that doesn't mean that the end result won't be satisfactory. Where the skier sees that he can *make* the skis turn at every step along the way, his motivation and desire to keep skiing will remain strong throughout the course.

In the second place, the initial explosive action coming from the mid-muscles of the body supplies the power for almost the entire turn. This "active" turning power constitutes what I call "direct turning," as opposed to the classic long carved turns, where the skier relies a great deal on the S and G forces to power the turn,

once the initial kickoff is supplied. This is "passive turning."

Direct turning is much simpler than the delicate business of getting just the right amount of edge on a ski so that it will carve nicely into a long passive turn. Thus, the Taylor system begins with the short, direct turns (which we have learned to call wedel turns). Since these are the easier turns, the Taylor system starts with a pat advantage over systems teaching long turns of any kind.

Now, on to the Taylor sequences themselves.

The Taylor system starts out on two-and-a-half-foot skis, goes on to four-foot skis, then five-foot skis, and finally back to the skier's own skis, if he owns any, or onto the longest rental skis he feels comfortable in handling. It is a method of teaching on skis the lengths of which graduate upward. At Killington, Vermont, and elsewhere, it is called the "Graduated Length Method." (Picture 73.) Taylor now teaches it at Squaw Valley, California.

The fine thing about the short-ski turn is that it can be practiced indoors. The skier takes a small rug and stands on a smooth floor; he can even do it in stockinged feet. He stands with arms out to the sides and twists his feet back and forth in rapid succession. The demonstrator here is Clif Taylor himself, ordinarily much happier-looking (Picture 74). His system and his skis (he designed his own to go with the system) have attracted the attention of commercial recreation specialists, and he is now allied with Northland Skis, a subsidiary of Larsen Industries of Minneapolis. Northland is backing Taylor's skis and his system.

Getting back to the indoor exercise, there are some important things to notice about it.

The "back and forth in rapid succession" signals that the reverse motion has to be used. This continuous twisting can only be done by reverse power. The twisting, once started, is carried on for a considerable time. The skier must get rhythm, as in a dancing lesson. At each beat he makes a twist "left-right." And then "right-left." It goes "left-right, right-left, left-right," and so on.

73

74

THE EXTENDED ARMS

Another important thing is the holding of the arms to the sides. This may seem insignificant, but it is a vital part of the system. Let's look at this for a minute.

The mid-muscles of the body in the "twist," or reverse motion, are forcing the feet and the upper body to turn opposite each other. This is the way it has to be. The skier can't twist the feet without a reverse motion in the upper body, and vice versa. The feet *must* turn in one direction (assuming there's not too much friction under them) when the upper body turns explosively in the opposite direction. There simply is no way of turning the feet or the skis without turning the upper body, either, when you are on a slope; it works both ways. The only way to avoid it is to have something to hold onto that could give you leverage on the snow.

If, for instance, the skier could grab a handy door frame with both hands, he could twist the feet *without* moving the upper body in space. He would be able to twist the feet much harder, too, since all the muscle could be directed to the feet and none would be used to turn the upper body.

Extending the arms to the sides is, in effect, like grabbing a door frame. The outstretched arms increase the resistance of the upper body to being turned (not quite as much as a door frame would, of course). With the arms increasing the resistance of the upper body to turning, more of the muscle force goes to turning the feet and the skis. In other words, with the arms out, the skis will turn that much more easily.

Of course, you have to do your bit to keep the skis friction-free. In more advanced long ski turns, the skis are simply jumped off the snow a bit, or unweighted. However, with short skis it is enough to keep them good and flat and perhaps to bounce a little, gently, up and down, as one twists.

75

76

77

78

There is no question that one has to work at it. There *is* friction between snow and ski.

Back to the rug situation: the rug also has some friction.

One important thing to notice about the rug exercise is the mental emphasis on twisting the feet. Concentration on turning the feet makes the feet turn more powerfully. There is nothing magic about this. It is simply that, in order to turn the feet effectively, the twist motion has to be started "explosively." Then the friction resistance is overcome right away. The feet turn as soon as the muscles act. Concentrating on moving the feet is a way of starting the movement "explosively."

So much for the rug.

When the skier is at the point in the rug exercise where he can make ten or twenty turns back and forth without interruption, he is ready to go outdoors.

By comparing Pictures 75 and 76, the reader can see that the movement is just the same, indoors or out.

The skier gets on a pair of two-and-a-half-foot skis and picks a well-packed spot on the flat. It should be good and hard. In fact, "boilerplate" snow is about the best thing to have for the first Taylor exercise outdoors.

79

TWISTING IN PLACE

Once the skier is in place with his two-and-a-half-footers, he starts his twist motion. He moves the ski tips: left-right-left. The resistance of snow is much greater, naturally, than that of a slippery floor. The twist motion has to be definitely *much more* explosive in order to achieve any turning of the skis at all. The skier *must* hold his arms out to the sides horizontally, or the exercise won't work very well. (Pictures 77 and 78.)

Two more things will help the skier to move the skis back and forth evenly. The first is pressing the knees and boots together. This provides a solid support for the skier and allows

80

81   82

him to turn the skis together, rather than one after the other.

The second is a *slight* bounce (not a hop). Complete unweighting is not needed here. But a slight, regular bounce aids the rhythm of the skier and reduces friction under the ski. The bounce should be timed so that the skier is *up* when the skis start moving through the arc. He comes *down* for a fraction of a second as the skis stop at the end of each arc. It is "up and twist" (Picture 77) and "down and stop" (Picture 78). Notice in Picture 78 that Taylor has a slight knee bend. He has come down from his bounce and is ready to bounce again.

If the snow is soft, the skis will dig themselves down after a number of arcs. This makes it harder to turn. The skier, therefore, should move to a new, smoother spot.

If the weight is too far forward, the skis will turn hard, and the same if the weight is too far back. The skier should move his weight back and forth over his skis until he finds the spot over the skis where the skis turn the most easily. If the weight is centered over the middle of the running surface of the ski, as it should be, the skis will make a neat hourglass pattern in the snow. The tips and tails of the skis each make their own separate little arcs in the snow, while the centers of the skis stay pretty much in place. This is what makes the hourglass pattern. (Pictures 79 and 80.) The top and bottom of the hourglass pattern will be about the same size if the weight is centered. If the arc at the tip of the skis is largest, the weight is too far back, and if the arc at the tail of the skis is largest, the weight is too far forward.

If the skier mounts bindings on his own skis, or even if a shop mounts them, he has to watch for the position of the boot on the ski. The ball of the foot (widest part of the boot) should be over the *center* of the running surface of the ski. The running surface is the flat part of the ski in contact with the snow. If the boots are mounted too far back on short skis (common in many cases), the skier will have to lean too far forward to get his weight centered. If he is mounted too far forward, the skier will have to sit back too far.

There are two good exercises for this outdoor short-ski practice. The first is to have another skier grasp the hands of the skier who is trying to twist in place. This gives the solid support necessary to get the skier started in the rhythm. (Picture 81).

The second, which is another way of increasing the skier's leverage, is simply to stick two poles in the snow. The skier uses them in the same way he might use another skier's hands,

83

84

to help him get started with the twist. However, if either or both bridging sequences are used, the skier should get back to the main exercise of twisting in place, using only his outstretched arms to help him stabilize the upper body.

Poles are normally not used in the short-ski technique until the skier is on the longest skis

that he is going to be using for a while. The reason for this is that the pole interferes with learning the twist down the hill. It is too easy for the skier to stick poles into the snow while he is going down the slope. He is trying to brake himself with the poles instead of relying on the braking effect of the turns. Poles can completely

skier turning

skier traversing

85

legs need not be together

86

87

disrupt the necessary rhythm of the Taylor system.

The skier should do the twist in place until he can make ten turns back and forth without stopping. The idea is to build up the feel for rhythm and balance on the short skis before taking them down the slope (Picture 82). In the Taylor method, this is where the skier gets his "reverse-motion reflex" built up. Thirty minutes of twisting in place on the snow is probably enough for most skiers; less might be too little. The twisting should be continued until it is almost automatic, like the steps of a dance. The dance simile is not so far wrong if we think of the beautiful coordination of a wedel skier on the slopes.

TWISTING DOWN THE SLOPE

The next thing the skier does is to practice the twist while he is going down the slope. (Pictures 83 and 84.)

This is a transition, since the skier has to take into account his speed down the hill, but with the two-and-a-half-footers, the speed is not very great. Usually the first turns come easily. (Picture 85.) To balance and twist properly, the skier must keep his arms out to the sides, a subtle but necessary item. The arms should be held out in a loose, relaxed manner, the wider the better (Picture 86), but not stretched to the last inch.

The skier must keep his skis fairly flat on the snow during the twist. Preferably, he should squeeze his skis and knees together, although if it is more comfortable for him to take a wider stance and separate the skis a bit, for stability, that is all right, too. The skier need not emphasize form at this point. It is more important that he twist the skis in a series of turns. It is surprising the extent to which the action of gravity, added to the simple twisting motion, will produce a series of turns, once the skier actually makes these twists as he drops. (Picture 87.) It is necessary at this point, however, that the skier start his twist explosively. Otherwise he will just be "steering" the small skis back and forth across the hill in long turns. This kind of steering doesn't lead to parallel skiing. Long, steered turns on short skis waste the great potential of the short ski for teaching the skier parallel. The short ski turns should be short, fast, and with a flat ski.

A problem will show up at this stage—"catching the outside edge." When the skier is making a turn with fairly flat skis, the edge of the ski on the outside of the turn runs the danger of catching in the snow, and the skier trips himself. The skier *will* catch some outside edges to

88

begin with, in the very nature of things, but falls on two-footers are not serious (Picture 88), and the skier will soon learn to keep the outside edge of the ski up just a bit. This is usually instinctive. If his falls keep recurring, the skier may have to concentrate actively on edging the ski a bit, bending the knee in toward the inside of the turn. Or he may have to keep the skis apart at first.

The terrain for the first short-ski exercise should be gentle, of course, with a flat runout at the bottom so that the skier will come to a stop by himself if he doesn't succeed in making good turns on the very first run. The snow should be fairly hard, and it is worth the effort to pack it out, if it is soft. This, again, is a crucial step in the system. Once the skier can make turns on a packed slope, he can make them in soft snow. Once he builds his confidence in his ability to make the ski turn, he can do it almost anywhere under any conditions, but the first turns have to be successful to give him confidence.

A packed slope will reduce the number of caught edges considerably. So will holding the skis a bit farther apart. But, as I have said, a few falls on short skis is nothing. They only reassure the skier that he can fall without harm. They take away the skier's fear of the skis and of falling, a major psychological victory.

The skier should not try to make too many corrections in his skiing at this stage. One practical advantage of the short skis is that so many factors can be ignored. The skier can put his entire attention on making the turns. He goes on. He gets his corrections later, when he has a bit more experience and when, above all, he *knows* he is going to be able to ski, so that corrections don't seem to be a life-or-death matter. The two-and-a-half-foot-ski learner doesn't even need to keep his skis together at first if he feels most stable with them apart. He can turn the skis simultaneously just as easily if they are six inches apart as when they are edge to edge, once he gets the hang of the turning. A distance between the skis is also a help in keeping the outside edges clear.

89

90

91

92

The thing the skier *does* need to watch is his fore-and-aft balance. He must stand *over* his boots or very nearly so. If he leans too far forward, the skis will nose in. If he leans back, they will get away from him. However, an over-the-boots stance is something that he automatically learns right away. It is mostly a question of learning to "stand up straight" without any other refinements. All this assumes that the bindings are properly mounted on the skis.

A common fault to avoid is "arm-waving."

Many skiers attempt to "steer" the skis with the arms. This amounts to a "rotation" type of turn. The arms should stay out at the sides; they should not be moved forward to start the turn. The turn should start in the movement of the lower body, which kicks the skis into the turn.

Apart from these considerations, the skier does not have to get into much detail about body position or anything else. As long as he makes *short* turns, he should be satisfied. Stopping to correct faults when the turns are going well is *wrong*, because it throws away the most precious advantage of short-ski learning: the chance to build up reverse reflex and balance and feel for the skis while *under way*. The skier who stands around in class watching others is wasting his time at this stage. He should be out experiencing his reactions to the skis, logging some mileage and stopping to correct only if he is not able to continue making short turns.

SHORT TURNS

The turns should not be long carved turns, as in Picture 89. This is fine for experienced skiers, but the beginner needs to stick with the idea of connecting short turns, as in Picture 90. The turns *must* be short, and to do this, the skis must be kept flat, so that they slew around. If the skier finds that he cannot do this readily, he needs some practice sideslipping. He may have to learn to flatten the ski to make slipped or slewed turns.

The first day on short skis should see the skier concentrating on skiing down the hill. If

93

94

95

he can get a few miles under his belt, other things will come much more easily. On this day his whole attitude toward the sport is being formed. If the first day's work is worrisome and painful, the skier's mental set toward skiing will be negative and it will take a lot for him to regain a positive attitude. If, on the other hand, he has a wonderful time, he will be able to

96

endure a lot of detailed correcting later on without getting impatient with himself or his teacher. He *knows* skiing is fun.

This concept of learning, incidentally, is a basic psychological concept that extends even to animals: the learning processes should be connected with pleasure, if the learning is to proceed well. In training a Seeing Eye dog, for instance, the trainer makes sure that the young puppy has plenty of play and very little training. If a Seeing Eye dog is taken into strict training in puppyhood, he becomes a balky, unmanageable adult dog.

Another thing to remember is that the whole process of learning to ski is to a certain extent outside the voluntary control of the skier. No matter how much of a "natural" he is, it takes a given amount of time for his motor reflexes to build up and for his mind to develop satisfactory sensitivity to the right "feel," particularly in regard to balance and edging. The more fun the skier has, the faster the reflexes build up, because a skier who is having fun is a skier willing to go up and down the slopes all day long and take his small mishaps in stride. The active, moving skier gets the needed experience much faster than his cousin who stands and watches others. This is true even though the cousin may be inherently better coordinated.

The only serious drill that the short ski pupil needs, outside the twist motion, is to learn to hold the turn so that he is heading across the hill and can easily come to a stop. This is something he should feel able to do. (Pictures 91 and 92.) Turning to a horizontal traverse and stopping gives the skier a chance to rest.

The beginning skier on two-foot skis often can go up the lift at a ski area within an hour of first getting on the skis. This is not true of the skier who starts on long skis; rather, it should not be true. (Self-taught beginners sometimes get on a lift long before they even begin to get used to their long skis, with very bad results.)

For the short-ski learner, the lift makes it possible to cover a great deal of territory.

Before he goes up the lift, however, the skier should spend a bit of time climbing up and twisting down. The climbing is a very good exercise and develops an instinctive feel for the skis.

Climbing on short skis is not a problem. The skier can side-step the skis up the hill simply by putting enough edge on the skis and putting them down firmly, sideways into the slope; the skis will bite in and hold. (Picture 93.)

Or, he can herringbone up the hill. To do this, he faces uphill and walks up in a knock-kneed position, putting the weight on the inside edges of the skis so they bite into the hill. (Pictures 94 and 95.)

The same climbing steps are used for long skis as well.

Short skis often work out very well for small skiers. They find it easier to climb up and ski down with two-and-a-half-foot skis than with the longer ones. Long skis mean using the snowplow, which is not so easy for the younger set. (picture 96.)

Chapter 6

LONGER SHORT SKIS

How the skier graduates to longer skis and starts making longer turns

In this chapter we see how the Taylor system connects with all other systems, including the American, Foeger, and Canadian.

The advantage of the short-ski systems is that today people who want to ski are not as serious as they were five or ten years ago, on the average. They want to learn, but they also want to enjoy it *soon*. They have been promised they *will* enjoy it by countless magazine, radio, and TV pronouncements. They may largely be lost to the sport in the long run if ski schools and learning systems do not take them into consideration. The short-ski idea is made for such people.

One reason for the potentially fast progress on short skis, besides the simplicity of the sequences and bridging sequences, is that the skier need never lose control. Once he learns to connect short turns, he can keep his speed down without any problem, assuming he stays on fairly moderate slopes. The skier who starts on long skis often finds he has to sit down to stop. This builds up a whole set of bad reflexes. It is all right to fall, but sitting down is a way of learning how not to ski. An unpremeditated fall, on the other hand, is not a set of learned reflexes.

Before a skier has conquered the twist on the two-footers and can go on, we must consider the bridging sequences to four-footers. In the Taylor

system, there are fewer than in others, but their function can be clearly seen.

The first bridging sequence teaches the skier to keep his skis closer together. As we have noted, this is not crucial with two-foot skis.

BRIDGES TO FOUR-FOOT SKIS

In the first exercise, the skier puts a glove between his knees, and twists down the hill squeezing the glove. This makes the skier keep the knees close together, and the skis consequently will be closer too.

The next exercise teaches the skier that he can twist his skis by using different portions of the body. First, he goes down the slope twisting the skis with a small twitch at the ankle. This makes a series of turns of very small arc. (Picture 97.) Then he goes down twisting the entire legs from thigh on down. This makes a series of slightly larger turns. Finally, he goes down the slope twisting the whole lower body from the waist down, making bigger turns. (Picture 98.) In the subsequent lessons, as the skis get bigger, the skier may find he has to make longer, bigger turns to get the skis moving in a rhythm of turns.

The third bridging exercise is to pick up one ski and twist down the hill on the other. This improves the balance, and the skier will become conscious of the fact that the weight can go on either ski.

The last bridging exercise is bouncing. The bounce, which the skier may or may not have used in his early twisting on two-footers, is necessary with the four-footers. The skier should practice bouncing as he goes down the slope on two-footers, with an "up" as he starts to twist and a "down" as he ends the twist. It will make for smoother skiing on the twos and build up the rhythm on the fours.

Bouncing does *not* mean that the skier hops

the same sequences on the two-footers that other skiers make on four-footers. They stay with their class, which is much more satisfactory than being left behind.

TWISTING ON FOUR-FOOTERS

The four-foot sequence starts off in much the same way as the two-foot sequence. The skier takes his four-footers out to a flat hard-snow surface and goes into the twist. (Pictures 99 and 100.) The skis will have to be twisted harder,

97

98

the skis in the air. Hopping is hard to do on short skis and will hold the skier back. One purpose of the short ski is to eliminate the need for the hop. To add a hop adds an unnecessary difficulty and lengthens the whole process of learning on short skis.

Assuming that the skier is anxious to get on to the longer skis and finally to American-system parallel, the two-foot stage should not take more than two days. A good skier can manage with one day. At the end of that day, he will be able to get down a beginning intermediate slope.

A certain proportion of skiers, perhaps one out of eight, will not be able to go on to four-footers immediately. They will need more work on the two-footers. However, they can go on making

because the resistance of the four-footer is about three times that of the two-footer. Even then, this resistance can be overcome by the skier if he gives the twist a real explosive action, together with a little bouncing up and down. The skier does not lift the skis off the snow. He brushes the skis back and forth on the snow. (Pictures 99 and 100.)

The skier who has trouble in twisting can use another skier's hands or his poles, as in the two-footer sequence, to get started.

Next, the skier takes the four-footers down the slope. (Pictures 101 and 102.)

Again, he will have to bounce more and twist harder. He should think more than he has about twisting the skis farther, to give him brak-

99

ing power, because the four-footers are faster than the twos.

He should also think more about getting his knees and skis together. This is the time to improve the edge control a bit, and getting the skis somewhat closer together calls for better edge control. He can consciously squeeze his knees and skis together in the turns. (Picture 103.)

But above all, he should stay with the concept of the connected turns, and let nothing interrupt that idea.

The skier will find that the four-footers give him more of the "real ski" feeling. He has more chance to lean forward when he starts down steep slopes (leaning forward helps the balance at this point) and he will find that sitting back makes it easier to go through deep snow. (Picture 104.)

The skier should consciously lean forward when the slope gets a bit steeper. This keeps

100

101

102

103

knees
together
in the
turn

skier can start to work a bit on his comma position. The comma at this point is an easy way of weighting the outside ski. The knees bend in, the shoulders lean over the outside ski and the skier takes the "reverse position" in the turn. (Picture 105.) The skier practices the comma in the turn to get weight on the outside ski.

Sometime during the second weekend, or possibly the third weekend, if he is skiing weekends, the skier will go onto five-foot skis.

FIVE-FOOT SKIS

This starts, as with the other stages, by a twist in place. (Picture 106.) The resistance of the five-footer is somewhat greater, but, surprisingly, not that much greater, than the resistance of the four-footer. But the skier *must* increase his twist force and also the *vigor* of the bouncing. It is especially important to start the turn quickly, explosively.

the skis from getting away from him. If the snow is soft, or if a sudden stop is necessary, he can sit back a bit.

The four-foot stage should take another day or two. The idea is to push toward longer skis all the way through. The skier should not get *too* comfortable on his shorter skis, because there are rewards in going on to the longer ones: more speed, better ride, and faster runouts.

There are several bridging sequences from four-foot skis to the five-foot skis.

There are, first, the different kinds of turns: twisting at ankle, leg, and waist. There is the one-ski twist.

Following the one-ski twist, the skier concentrates on getting the weight on the outside ski of the turn. This becomes important now. It is quite possible to ski four-footers without having the weight on the outside ski. But practice in leaning on the outside ski is needed to progress to the fives. This is the point where the

sitting
back
in
deep
snow

104

105

Once the skier can make ten or more turns in a row, back and forth in place, with the five-footer, he can then take them down the slope. At this point, some skiers may have difficulty and should go back to the four-footers for another day or two. This is perfectly fine. The skier on four-footers can still follow along in class with the skiers doing five-foot exercises. He will work up to the five-footers eventually.

The five-footers should be used on the same easy slopes as the fours. The same concept of

107

connected turns holds here. (Picture 107.) It is imperative that the skier work on his rhythm in the turns. Otherwise he will lose the valuable reflexes of the reverse motion he has built up and will lose the feeling for the wedel turn. The turns will not, of course, be quite as short, because the skis are longer. But the turns should be made as short as possible. If the skier does not connect his turns, it is usually because he is *not* keeping the skis *flat* enough at the start of

106

the turn and through the turn. Or it is because he does not *bounce* enough.

If the skier has trouble making short turns on five-footers, he should first go into some side-slip practice, to get the feel of flattening the ski. (Picture 108.) Then he should practice his bounce.

He must also try to work on his comma, so that he gets his weight to the outside ski in the turn. Otherwise, at the five-foot length, the skis will tend to cross or split. There is a very good exercise for this, and that is to lift the tail of the inside ski at the end of the turn. (Picture

sidesslipping

108

109.) If the skier is good enough, he can lift the ski earlier and earlier in the turn, using more and more comma to do it. This is the way toward the long-ski turn.

Lastly, he should bounce into the turns. At this stage, if he wishes, he can hop the tails just a bit to start the turn. The tip of the ski should stay on the snow, however.

The five-foot ski, let it be said, is a *real* ski. Not only are there wooden five-footers available, but there are metal five-footers, made by Head and by Hart. Skiers who get to the five-foot stage and feel that this is the longest ski they want to handle might think of buying either the Head or the Hart five-footer. The metal ski is inherently an easier ski to handle and takes the bumps and dips much more easily than the wooden ski.

Progress from here on is up to the skier. He can try six-footers next, using the same techniques to get a short turn, and go on to sevens, if he is eager to try them. Each added length gives the skier better handling characteristics. But each added length also calls for more

bounce, or lift, more weight shift to the outside ski, and more edge control.

We have left the matter of edge control to the last in the Taylor system. But once the skier is on the ski that he feels is the right length for him, he will want to go on to steeper slopes. This, of course, is the fun of it. There are always more challenges.

But the flat-ski slewed turn, which is what we have been talking about in these two chapters, is not suitable for the steeper stuff. Now the skier has to think about putting his skis on edge.

EDGING SKIS

Edging means braking power, and braking power is what steep slopes call for.

It is important to remember here that the ski, even on steeper slopes, has to be flat at the start of the turn. It is edged later in the turn. You cannot twist an edged ski into the turn to start the turn.

However, with a judicious bending-in of the knees, the skier can put his skis on edge through

lifting the inside ski in the turn

109

bending knees to edge skis in a turn

110

The tip of the "following (downhill) ski" will hold the uphill ski in place. It is clear that the reverse position makes it easier to lead with the uphill ski, because the reverse position causes the uphill side of the body to advance.

This idea of lead is also part of turning. The skier who is making a carved turn has to make sure that the comma position includes advancing the inside ski of the turn. When turns are connected, there is a "change of lead." In a turn to the right, the right ski is inside and that ski leads. In a turn to the left, the left ski leads. (Pictures 112 and 113.) This keeps the skis from crossing in the turn.

The traverse position and the change of lead are introduced much later in the short-ski system than in other systems. In the flat-ski twist of the first short-ski stages, the change of lead takes place almost automatically, because of the use of the reverse motion. On the five-foot-ski level, it does become desirable to change lead consciously. This is particularly so when the skier tries for the longer, carved turn. The longer the turn, the more likely the skis are to start crossing.

the last three quarters of the turn, increasing the amount of edging as the turn continues and achieving much more braking power. He is working toward the expert's carved turn. (Picture 110.)

The best way to practice bending-in, or "angulation," is to practice the traverse position, which is the same on short skis as it is in the American system. The traverse position is the comma position, with more reverse and more inward bend at the knees angulation as the slope gets steeper. The more angulation, the more edging the skis gets. (Picture 111.)

The reversed position of the shoulders makes it easier for the skier to bend at the waist, as well. The bend at the waist is used to get the weight of the shoulders over the downhill ski. In the traverse position, the skier must get his weight on the downhill ski solidly, otherwise the downhill ski will slip and split away from the uphill ski.

The other thing that the traverse position introduces is the idea of "lead ski." The uphill ski must be advanced about six inches. This keeps the uphill ski from crossing the downhill ski.

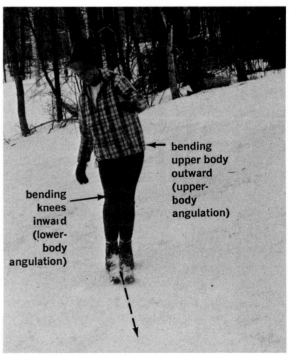

bending upper body outward (upper-body angulation)

bending knees inward (lower-body angulation)

111

left ski
leading

112

right
ski
leading

113

In the short-ski system, also, the skier holds off learning the traverse until he has really gotten the idea of connecting his turns on longer skis. Once learned, the traverse position is a stable position, and the skier can use it to cross any hill with admirable control, without side-slipping (Picture 114). It is a nice, easy thing to do—too easy, in fact. The skier will find that he wants very much to hold this safe and stable position, and if he gets used to it too early in his learning process, he will find that his muscles refuse to flatten the ski and go slipping naturally through the reverse turns. The "traverse habit," or "traversitis," can become a major block to progress.

Technically, every full, long turn starts and ends in the traverse position. This is all well and good. But the beginning skier finds it hard to flatten his skis and come out of this position for the next turn, even with unweighting. In the short-ski system, until the very end, then, he doesn't worry about traverse. He is engaged in a series of turns with the skis fairly flat and he stays on moderate slopes. The result is that he twists from one turn to the next without trouble.

The short-ski system is fairly new. Some ski schools, notably the Killington and Bolton Valley schools in Vermont, are experimenting intensively with the system, using it along with regular classes on long skis as an alternative way of teaching. As more schools try it, we should be getting more and more efficient short-ski exercises and faster progress.

114

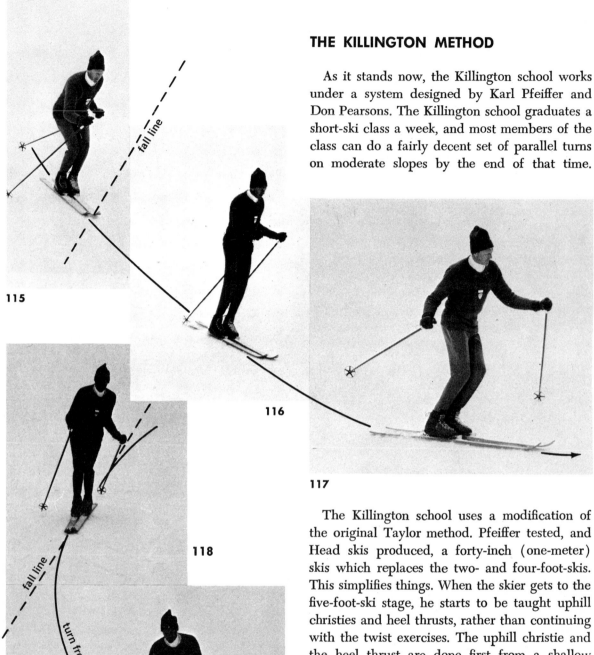

115

116

117

118

119

THE KILLINGTON METHOD

As it stands now, the Killington school works under a system designed by Karl Pfeiffer and Don Pearsons. The Killington school graduates a short-ski class a week, and most members of the class can do a fairly decent set of parallel turns on moderate slopes by the end of that time.

The Killington school uses a modification of the original Taylor method. Pfeiffer tested, and Head skis produced, a forty-inch (one-meter) skis which replaces the two- and four-foot-skis. This simplifies things. When the skier gets to the five-foot-ski stage, he starts to be taught uphill christies and heel thrusts, rather than continuing with the twist exercises. The uphill christie and the heel thrust are done first from a shallow traverse. (Pictures 115–117.)

Next in the Killington five-foot stage, the skier starts making christies and heel thrusts from steeper and steeper traverses, and finally doing the heel thrust from the fall line.

The heel thrust is lengthened into a long carved turn with plenty of edging. In the end, the skier has a pretty good long carved turn, with lots of speed on moderate terrain and going from one steep traverse to another (Pictures 118 and 119).

The danger in making longer turns at the five-foot stage is that the skier loses his feeling for the short, flat-ski connected turns. The Killington system is working toward the American system at an earlier stage than the Taylor system. This means that it *has* to run the risk of the skier's losing the "connected-turn feeling." But, once the skier has acquired the carved turn, he can go more easily into the American system, because the American parallel turn is built on carved turning.

RENTING SHORT SKIS

One disadvantage of the short-ski system is that each skier has to have a number of pairs of skis available.

The Killington school owns its own stock of Head one-meter and Head five-foot skis. This solves the problem of the skier's getting short-ski lengths for himself. In some other circumstances, he will have to supply his own lengths of short skis. Some rental shops at the various ski areas have a stock of varying lengths. But the skier may have to *buy* his own. This makes it somewhat more expensive by the time he is all the way through to six- or seven-foot skis, but he gains time, which is also worth money. And he has more fun, which is the idea in the first place. The skiers who have outgrown their shorter skis often sell them or lend them to friends who want to start out. There is a seller's market in short skis these days.

This writer had stopped taking beginning skiers with him; he only resumed taking them again with the advent of short skis. If you have a beginning skier with you and put him on long skis, you will be forced to watch him all day long or pay the ski school to do it. Put the beginning skier on two-footers, and you can start him twisting and then, after an hour, let him go on his own.

At some point in the short-ski sequence, the skier should start using poles. This should come when he has confidence in making connected turns without the pole; having reached that stage, he will not use the pole to stop himself or to "pry" himself into the turn. "Hanging on the poles" to force the turn to start can be a major beginner's problem. But once the skier can take his poles along without letting them interfere with his skiing, they are a decided advantage. For one thing, they act as extensions of the arms, giving the upper body more stability and making it easier to turn the feet *more* and the upper body *less*. For another, the poles are very nice to rest on and to use when the skier is walking across the flat or climbing.

When the skier comes to making the long ski turns, he will use the pole to "mark" the turn, jabbing it in lightly when he starts his bounce to unweight the skis. When he tries steeper slopes, the poles assume a more important role. He plants a pole and "rides over" it to help him get a real hop and start the turn quickly.

To sum up the short-ski system, we can safely say that the skier at the end of a week's work will have accomplished a great deal in terms of technique. He will also have found his proper length of ski. When he gets a ski that is too long, he'll know it, because he won't be able to handle it; he'll be glad to drop back a length for the time being, so that he can have fun.

From here the path leads directly into the beginning parallel class of the American system. The skier will find he is capable of doing the beginning parallel sequences on moderate slopes. He will eventually want to learn the snowplow, stem, and stem christie turns, because these are good turns to have. In many special situations on long skis these turns work better than parallel: in a narrow corridor, or when the skier has to carry a load down the hill, such as another pair of skis or a pack, or has to come to a stop in a crowded situation. By this time, however, he is in no danger of getting permanently stuck at the stem-turn level. He has learned by the most up-to-date method available the direct-turn, direct-parallel, "Graduated Length Method" system.

Chapter 7

NATUR TEKNIK

The Foeger system of parallel turning on long skis from the beginning

Now we come to the original teacher of "direct parallel." Walter Foeger's Jay Peak, Vermont, school has been copied (with Foeger's approval) in many schools in the East. Foeger conducted his own certification of instructors for these schools, just as PSIA does for the American-system schools through the PSIA regional organizations. Foeger is one of the genuine innovators in the history of ski-school systems.

Foeger's system has been going·as long as the American system, and there has been an obvious underground reaction between the two. Who copied whom is beside the point; the point is to teach the skier how to ski.

Foeger's method is built around the "ski week." People take a vacation, have lessons every day, and by the end of this time, achieve a certain level of competence. Now the Foeger school guarantees that you *will* ski parallel (on moderate slopes) by the end of the ski week, or it will return your money. His is the only ski school that makes such an offer.

The Foeger schedule, however, is *two* classes a day, instead of the usual one. The school can handle only half as many skiers per instructor; and there is a heavier demand on the courage and endurance of the pupil than other systems: Foeger feels that the skiers respond to the challenge.

Foeger divided his system into eight stages. The bridging sequences are worked out in de-

tail. All Foeger schools follow them quite closely. (The PSIA system, by contrast, allows the bridging sequences, or "method," to be made by the individual ski school.)

120. *Walter Foeger in a parallel turn.*

THE FIRST STAGE

Foeger's first stage is called "Basic Exercises." There are about thirty. Not all the exercises available at each stage are used by every Foeger teacher in every class. The exercises are there if the teacher feels that the skiers need it.

The objective of the first stage is "balance and familarity with the skis."

First, the skier stands in place, lifts one ski tail, then the other. He bends at the knees, straightens. He hops the tails of both skis. (This is a preparation for unweighting.) He swings one ski out to the side, holds the ski horizontal, and balances on the remaining ski. (This is a preparation for "skating.") Then he translates some of these exercises to the moving-down-the-slope situation.

The skier will now start running straight down the slope (known as "schussing"). For his first run, the skier simply lets the skis come to a stop naturally at the end of the run. Then he makes another "schuss," picking up the tail of one ski and then the other as he runs. (Picture 121.) Next, he skis down while bending and straightening the knees. Next, he skis down while using the bending and straightening motion to hop both tails off the snow.

One effect of this excellent sequence is to keep the skier "loose" while skiing down the hill, a thoroughly good idea. Too many skiers freeze into a rigid position when they make their first downhill runs. This position deprives them of the chance to make quick movements of the body, particularly in the arms and legs, so that they can adjust their balance for slight variations in the terrain. Instead, they tend to fall to the

121

snow as if they were congealed. One of the essences of skiing is to stay loose enough to react gracefully to the unforeseen.

The straight running position of the Foeger skier is fairly erect. Foeger called it "resting on the bones." It means that, in the erect position, the skeleton takes the weight of the skier down through an erect backbone to the hipbones and down to the skis. The skier who hangs his upper body forward, obviously, is putting a great strain on the muscles of the back if he stays that way all the time.

THE SKATING STAGE

Foeger's second stage is called "skating." Foeger said of it: "It is hard to understand why

122

123. *Billy Kidd making a skating-step turn in the Stowe 1966 National races.*

the skating exercises are not used more in ski teaching. Skating under the instruction of a good teacher develops a tremendous amount of edge control, an understanding of change of direction and timing." (Actually, skating is quite widely used in the Canadian systems as a teaching method.)

In Foeger's system, the skier first skates on flat ground. This is not hard; the skier who makes up his mind to it, can do it. He has to launch himself over one ski, go forward with it in one direction, then point the other ski off a bit, go forward with it in a slightly new direction. He then does the same down a gentle slope that has a runout at the end. Next, instead of skating down the hill, he skates across the hill, skating up onto the higher ski, bringing the other ski up parallel, and then stepping up again onto the higher ski. The exercise is a skating-step turn. (Picture 122.)

Foeger pointed out that this exercise teaches the skier to "change edges." That is, the ski that the skier steps onto will naturally have the up-

124

hill edge rolled into the snow. When he steps off this ski, he will roll it onto its other edge, to give him enough traction to push. This *rolling* of the ski from one edge to a flat position and then onto the other edge is, in effect, a second, important phase of edge control. The skier who can feel just which edge is biting, or when the ski is flat, has learned an important lesson.

125

126

twist
upper body
to face left

original ski positions

hop in
circle
to
left

127

Before the skier is through with this stage, he will skate down the fall line and out of it, making, in effect, a skating turn up the hill.

THE TRAVERSE

The next stage finds the skier traversing.

The Foeger traverse is quite like the American method traverse, except that the skier's arms are held out a bit wider (true throughout the Foeger technique). The skier has a comma: reversed position, together with a leaning out from the knees and waist. (Picture 124.) The skier lifts the tail of one ski, lifts the tail of the other ski, bends, and straightens the knees. Then he hops both ski tails off the snow. Then he does these things in succession in the same traverse. (Picture 125.) These moves all further the ability to handle the skis separately and to "hop" the tails at any time. The emphasis on being able to move while in the traverse position is good. Skiers in a traverse tend to freeze

into a "picture position" and lose the ability to correct for changes in speed and terrain.

PREPARING TO TURN

The "Preparation Turn to the Mountain" is a crucial stage. Here the Foeger school introduces the reverse motion in earnest, together with a hop or unweighting motion.

The skier sticks a pole in the snow and stands with the tips of the skis at the pole. He then hops the tails of the skis to the left until he has at least partly circled the pole. (Pictures 126 and 127.) Then he does the same to the right. (Pictures 128 and 129.) As he jumps, he faces the direction of the jump, turning the upper body to do so. This exercise does two things. First, it raises the idea of *direction* in the hopping of the tails; it shows the skier he can hop the tails to either side as well as straight into the air. Second, it provides concentrated practice on the reverse motion. The upper body

128

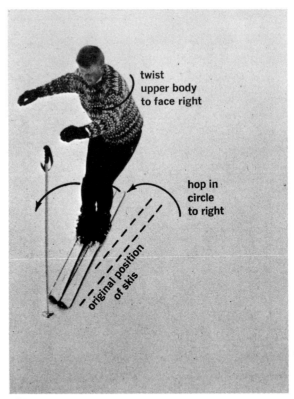

twist
upper body
to face right

hop in
circle
to right

original position
of skis

129

is turning one way while the skis are turning the other way. Hopping the tails to the left is, in effect, a movement that turns the ski tips to the right. Either way, it starts a right turn. The skier is, in effect, turning the skis right and turning his upper body to face left, which is the reverse movement.

After doing it in place, the skier does the hop-and-reverse in motion; he hops tails downhill from a traverse run, on an easy hill. He does it several times in rapid succession to make a sort of rough uphill turn.

It is a case of hopping the tails downhill to make the skis turn uphill, a sophisticated approach that most self-taught skiers don't arrive at by themselves. They strain to force the tips uphill instead, and that doesn't really work. (Incidentally, this repeated hop is a method by which expert skiers sometimes make a turn through heavy, wet snow in which the tails won't slide.)

The Foeger-system skier next makes hops that set the tails downhill as he goes over a sharp drop-off or mogul. The tails consequently slide a bit at each hop. The skier is now on the way to making an uphill christie.

THE SIDE SLIDE

Next in the Foeger system is stage five: the side slide, as he calls it, or the sideslip, as the rest of the world calls it. Side sliding was just as important to Foeger as the more famous hopping exercises. After all, hopping the tails to one side without having them slide is a very abrupt maneuver. The addition of the slide following the hop is what makes the hop valuable. The side slide is often wrongly regarded as something used by itself. The Foeger system connects the slide and the hop intimately, and thus stages four and five are a valuable one-two for the skier.

The side slide sequence is as follows.

The skier side-steps down the hill, in reversed position, so that he learns to face the bottom.

130

131

Then, after mounting to the top, he puts both poles behind him and pushes himself sideways down the hill. (Picture 130.) Then he tries it without using the poles, by flattening the skis. Next, he does the slide, bending the knees and straightening them as he slides, to keep relaxed and to help the process along.

The Foeger skier next does the "traverse side-sliding." This means sliding sideways and forward, so that he is going across the hill as well as down.

Then there is "stair sliding," which is, first, a side slide, and then putting skis on edge to make a short traverse (1 in Picture 131), and then another side slide (2 in Picture 131), and so on. This is a great edge control exercise; reminds the skier that he *must* consciously flatten the ski to side slide.

The skier in Foeger's sixth stage starts on a moderate hill, takes a shallow traverse, and then hops in an "up-and-forward" motion, moving the tails of the skis downhill, with the reverse motion, landing the skis fairly flat, slides them around to the horizontal traverse position. (Pictures 132 and 133.)

Now he does the same from a steep traverse. Note how the skier crouches in Picture 132, comes up in Picture 133, and starts the tails turning in the air (or just brushing the surface of the snow). At the end of the turn, the skier's position is "reversed" and he is facing downhill. (Picture 134.)

Next come the short turns, which are closer to heel thrusts: more explosive reverse movement, smaller hop. There is the heel thrust from the shallow traverse. (Picture 135.) Then, the skier makes the thrust from the diagonal and finally from the fall line. (Picture 136.)

All these started with a hop, or up-motion. This so-called "up-unweighting" is the way in which the Foeger system and the American system prepare for the heel thrust and uphill christie. In this they are closer to each other than to the Austrian system, in which the heel thrust and the uphill christie are executed in a single down-motion, without any preparatory up-motion.

132

133

134

In the uphill turn or uphill christie, the Foeger system has the skier on a traverse path, facing his tips, jumping the tails downhill as he reverses a *quarter turn* to face downhill. (Pictures 137 and 138.)

135

136

137

upper-body
quarter turn
hopping
tails
downhill

turn to come is
up the hill

138

139

upper-body
half turn
hopping
tails
uphill

turn to come is
down the hill

140

STARTING THE TURN DOWNHILL

In stage seven, "Preparation Turn Downhill," the basic exercise starts from a traverse position with the upper body reversed, facing the downhill side of the skis (Picture 139) as if he'd just finished an uphill christie. From this position, the skier jumps the ski tails uphill and reverses his upper body a *half-turn,* to face the fall line. This is the starting motion for a turn *down the hill,* in the direction that can be seen in Picture 140.

After he can hop the skis with a half-turn of the upper body at each hop, the Foeger skier goes on to the next exercise. This is alternating a half-turn left of the upper body with a half-turn right. The skis make the opposite motion. The tips turn left if the body turns right, and so on; here the motion of left and right becomes very much like the Taylor twist. The Foeger skier is hopping the full-length ski back and forth rather than twisting the short ski, but in both the Foeger hop and the Taylor twist the accent is on the actual, direct "twist" turning of the skis.

The Foeger school next has a series of exercises for continuing the skier's education in making the tips turn downhill.

In Picture 141, the skier is running down the slope in normal running position. In 142 he has crouched and is starting to come up. In 143, he is up but has not yet started his skis turning.

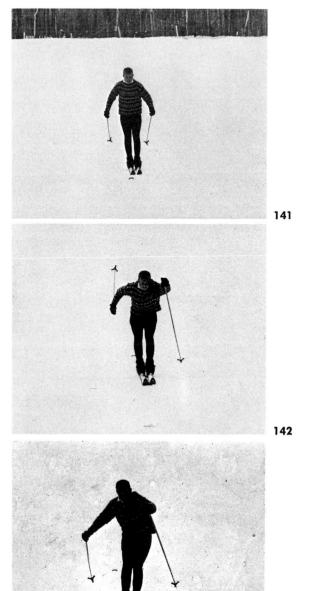

141

142

143

144

In 144, he has spun the skis with a reverse motion and is headed for the horizontal traverse line.

Picture 143 shows the Foeger counter-comma

position. The skier in the fall line makes a comma toward the inside of *the turn to come.* The counter-comma's function is to set the skier's body so that he can get a full half-turn for his reverse motion. This makes for a more powerful reverse motion of the upper body.

The Foeger skier next makes wedel hops in the fall line. This is a very fast back-and-forth hopping, with half-turns of the upper body left and right. Here it looks much more like the Taylor twist.

Now we go on to the next step.

The skier uses reverse upper-body motion combined with single hops of the tails uphill from a steep traverse.

Anytime you hop the tails of the skis *uphill,* you are starting a turn *down the hill.* The uphill hop of the ski tails makes the ski tips swing decisively *down the hill.* This is the essence of the *turn into the fall line.*

The Foeger skier first does a *stop turn* over a drop-off, to get a faster, better turn out of the fall line. The skier runs in the fall line and, with one hop and reverse (third figure from start in Picture 145), hops the skis part way around, and lets them slide the rest of the way, keeping his weight on the outside ski by means of the comma position. As the skis come around, the skier edges them more and more and finally edges them to a stop.

Before finishing up this stage, the Foeger skier goes back to the wedel exercise on steep slopes. At the end of stage seven, he can swing the skis downhill into the fall line by means of one, two, or three hops and make a very fast christie out of the fall line to a stop.

THE DOWNHILL TURN

Stage eight is the "Turn Downhill." There is emphasis on cutting down the number of hops. Once he has it down to two hops (one *to* the fall line and one to start the uphill christie) he is almost to the full parallel turn.

In the final phase of stage eight, the skier makes one hop of the tails from the traverse

145

toward the fall line, and the rest of the turn is slid. (Picture 146.) This hop is smoothed to fluid up-motion. The ski tails brush the snow rather than go off the snow. This is the final Foeger full parallel turn. (Pictures 147–152.)

What the skier has at the end of a Foeger week is a long parallel turn on a moderate slope, with some capability for shorter uphill christies and heel thrusts from the fall line.

Not every Foeger skier makes it this far in a week, but an amazing number seem to go a good deal of the way. Wherever the skier goes from here, he takes with him a good solid foundation for parallel turn.

A few find the Foeger method a bit too acrobatic and would rather go with a more slow-moving system as in the Austrian or American system. But, although Foeger's schools are on a money-back guarantee, very few people stop to collect their money at the end of a ski week: Foeger has said it is something like five or ten a year.

A few comments might be made on the Foeger system.

The first is the early introduction of the traverse. I would prefer to see the sideslip used here. Mine is a rather unorthodox idea: watch beginning parallel skiers. You will see that they obviously make better turns out of a forward sideslip than out of a traverse.

With great emphasis placed on the traverse,

146

147

148

the beginning skier tends to get "traversitis": the traverse is such a safe and easy way of going across the slope that skiers tend to stick to it, and they have trouble turning out of it.

Also, I see no advantage of mixing the long and the short turns. I suggest an experiment in this direction: short turns first, then long turns.

Another comment on the Foeger method: there is excessive emphasis on turning the upper body.

It is entirely possible to reverse the upper body without affecting the ski's direction one bit. It is only when the reverse motion is started *explosively* that the middle muscles of the body will turn both the upper body *and* the skis. Foeger skiers have a tendency (not in all cases,

of course) to turn the upper body but not the skis. Excess upper-body movement *can* throw the skier off balance, because there is no compensating turning movement in the skis. Unless the skis and the upper body turn at the same time, the dynamic balance of the reverse turn is lost.

The comments I offer are not intended to obscure the fact that Foeger's is the first successful system for direct parallel teaching. For this alone, Foeger deserves a niche in the history of ski teaching.

The future direction of "direct parallel" is indeed a challenge. As someone once said in another context, "We are faced with a series of magnificent opportunities brilliantly disguised as insoluble problems."

149

150

151

152

Chapter 8

THE AMERICAN SYSTEM

The system of the great tradition and what it can do for the skier

The American system is the "establishment," as far as American skiing goes. Like any big institution, the American system is constantly under attack. This is a measure of its success.

The selfless devotion of a good many instructors in this country produced the organization known as the Professional Ski Instructors of America, which in turn produced the American system. Before that, we had the Chaos system. Every school was a law unto itself, and there was no chance for good communication between the different United States schools. They didn't speak the same language.

Now the American technique is the common language of most of them. The bows for this accomplishment go to a number of fine ski-school heads. Paul Valar, as I have said, led the effort. Bill Lash of Utah was the first PSIA president and it was at his urging that the PSIA technical committee moved ahead. Other members were Willy Schaeffler, who ran our 1960 Olympics, Junior Bounous of California and Utah, and Max Dercum of Arapahoe Basin, Colorado.

The founding of the American system led to a revolution in our custom of looking toward Europe for the guidance of experts. When the Austrian wedel came out, there was no over-all national U.S. body of ski teachers capable of evaluating the new idea. It took over on the force of Kruckenhauser's recommendation and

153. *Paul Valar, head of the ski school at Cannon Mountain, New Hampshire, and of the Professional Ski Instructors technical committee, was instrumental in the shaping of the American system of ski teaching.*

the success of the Austrian racers. Not many skiers here even knew *how* to make the reverse motion. And what was taught as the "reverse turn" was often pretty much of a caricature of it.

Today, in the face of a similar situation, the PSIA is in position to evaluate any system by having certain ski schools work on it experimentally. If it is accepted, it will be presented thoroughly by proper methods.

THE STANDARD SYSTEM

The American system today is the standard by which other systems are judged. If a system claims the right to be recognized, it has to prove that it has advantages over the American system.

Likewise, any outside system has to dovetail with the American system, at some stage, because the goals of the American system are the long carved parallel turn and the carved wedel. So far no one has come up with better goals.

With a standard like the American system to go by, better skiing and better teaching have been the natural outcome. We have just begun to see this, but we can confidently look ahead to seeing the teaching methods become even more compact and efficient.

What we have now in the American system, with its standard stages of progress through snowplow, snowplow turn, and so on, is by far the most rigorous method of attaining parallel skiing yet devised. For those who stick it out, there is great reward. The skier who follows through on the American system comes out more thoroughly trained than he would be by any other method.

There is one powerful argument for going to parallel via the snowplow and stem route. The snowplow and stem are S- and G-powered: they depend on snow resistance and gravity. The skier who gets the feel of riding these forces has learned something irreplaceable. The American system gives the best training possible for getting this feel.

There is also a very practical consideration: the system gets the skier to do a turn in two days. Direct-parallel, long-ski schools such as Foeger's cannot yet do this—without using short skis.

The stages of the American system are eleven in number. Each stage culminates in a "look" or "final form," the ideal way to finish out each stage. Naturally the skier is not expected to *reach* the ideal in any one of these stages (it would take him too long to become that polished); only an *instructor* should be able to demonstrate the final form of each stage. This gives the skier a visible model to follow.

In the learning situation, a good instructor is satisfied if the pupil is able to approximate the final form in any of the early stages. The instructor does not worry whether or not the skier is picture-pretty; he wants the skier to get the basic idea, get on with it, and go on to higher stages.

The American system does not prescribe the bridging sequences for its ski schools. Individual ski-school heads do that. This leaves a great deal of discretion to the schools. Within the freedom allowed them, then, the various PSIA schools have developed widely varying sequences. Some of them have an elaborate set of exercises: Junior Bounous' schools are a good example of this.

The danger of not having enough sequences is that the skier will not be able to make it smoothly from stage to stage. He then will spend a lot of time trying to conform to a new position that he can't master. On the other hand, too many sequences will disperse the skier's effort and he will lose the sense of where he's going.

Quite a number of PSIA schools use hop sequences something like those used by Foeger. Other schools don't like the hop. Killington's Pearsons says that the hop brings the skier on his uphill ski too easily. These are typical of differences in *method* among American ski schools; it should be stressed that the *technique* or final form is the same.

THE AMERICAN SYSTEM BASICS

Now, to get down to the American system itself.

The straight-running position in the American system is the first stage. It is a "tall-in-the-saddle" look, with very little knee bend. (Picture 154.) The arms are relaxed and held close

154

skis more on edge. The edging is done with the bending-in of both knees as in angulation. (Picture 155.) The skier should stay quite relaxed and upright.

The danger of the snowplow is that the skier feels so safe that he stays in it and does not want to do any straight running.

Therefore, the method of good American schools stresses going from the running position into snowplow and back again. To do this, the skier in running position must "brush" the tails of the skis out to the sides as he moves forward.

155

to the sides down to the elbow, with the forearm holding the poles out to the sides and in front just a little.

The skier concentrates on staying loose and relaxed rather than on getting into a picture stance at this point.

Sequences used by various schools to improve the stance are aimed at keeping the skier from tightening up. These include the skier's going under a gate made of three slalom poles; picking up a glove from the snow; lifting one ski at a time; bouncing the tails of both skis in the air going down; bouncing without lifting the tails.

The second stage is the "straight snowplow."

This is a braking maneuver, as discussed in Chapter 1. It also teaches the skier elementary edge control.

The bridge sequences to the snowplow include several exercises. The skier can put both poles in the snow ahead of him, lean on them, step the skis into the snowplow position, and then take his weight off the poles to start the snowplow. This is the bridge most frequently used.

The edge control comes in when the skier wishes to control speed. He merely puts the

With too much edging, the skier won't be able to get into the plow. In closing the plow to the running position, the skier simply narrows the plow, squeezing his legs together.

The skier should avoid the idea that he can make sudden stops with the snowplow. He should practice it on a gradual slope and give himself plenty of time to stop. The snowplow is a slow-acting brake. Trying to make a fast stop will cause the skier to get into a cramped, over-edged position. The skier should not "freeze." He should bounce a bit as he goes

156

G →

← S

turn from fall line

157

158

159

original
traverse

turn from

G

shallow traverse

S

160

new traverse

161

inward
knee bend
edges skis

163

162

upper body
leans out

extreme
inward
knee bend

164

165

down, bend the knees, straighten them, and so on. He should shift his weight back and forth so that he finds a comfortable posture for himself.

THE SNOWPLOW TURN

The third stage is the snowplow turn.

Bridges to the snowplow turn include step turns (to learn the idea of turning across the hill), leaning down to touch the lower calf while in the snowplow (to get a start on the idea of weight shift).

The first snowplow turn is made from the fall line (Pictures 156 to 158). The theory is to increase the S and G forces on one ski by putting more weight on one ski. This ski becomes "the steering ski" as the S and G forces on this ski spin the skier around. Bending in the outside knee (the knee over the outside ski of the turn) and at the same time leaning out over the outside ski with the shoulders is helpful. In the American, the leaning out at the shoulders is called "upper-body angulation," and the bending-in of the knee is called "lower-body angulation."

In addition to angulation, the upper body assumes the reverse position (outside shoulder back) to help the skier to put more weight on the outside ski of the turn. The combination of reverse and angulation produces the American comma position.

The bending in of the knee is used to edge the ski on which the weight is, and consequently to give the ski turning and braking power. Proper edging of the ski (not too much to begin with) will give all the turning power necessary if the skier's weight is in the right place—just back of the center of the ski. The skier should not *twist* the outside ski around but should move his weight back and forth over it until he attains the position over the outside ski that creates the most noticeable turning effect. There must be sufficient separation of S and G forces, or they won't spin the ski. This means the weight has to be a bit back of center of the ski to separate S and G.

This is a completely S- and G-powered turn and is the basis for the S- and G-powered turns that the American system favors all the way through.

Once the skier can do one snowplow, he can do several in a row. At the end of one plow, since he is running in a traverse direction across the hill, he will have to turn from that traverse and come down into the fall line.

The final form of the snowplow turn is from the traverse direction. (Picture 159.) The skier holds the plow position as he traverses. Then he puts his weight on the *uphill* ski, and this ski becomes the outside ski at the turn and starts steering the skier toward the fall line. (Picture 160.) The skier who does not overedge but keeps a fairly flat ski at the beginning of the turn usually has an easier time getting the turn started out of the traverse direction and into the fall line.

The turn goes into the fall line and out again into the new traverse, going in the direction opposite the first turn. (Picture 161.)

As the skier comes out of the fall line, he must edge the lower ski a bit more than at the beginning, so that he gets a carved turn at the end and adds braking power.

Again, the turn does not depend at all on a mid-body muscle movement. The skier should try to get the sense of the ski turning itself. The ski is not twisted through the turn but is held out in the V position with the legs.

THE TRAVERSE

The next stage in the American system is the traverse, or moving across the hill. (Picture 162.)

In the American system traverse, the skier sets his edges hard enough into the hill so that the skis do not sideslip. The edges are set by the comma position: the knees bend in toward the hill, the shoulders lean out away from the hill, and the lower shoulder is drawn back somewhat. (Picture 163.)

168   167   166

Exercises to improve the traverse include lifting the tail of the uphill ski to make sure that the weight is mainly on the downhill ski; bouncing to stay loose; exaggerating the reverse of the upper body by pointing the navel downhill, and touching the calf of the downhill leg with the downhill hand to exaggerate the bend at the waist and get more weight on the downhill ski.

The steeper the slope, the greater the bend at knee and waist. The skier must lean *down* the hill to make a good traverse on a steep hill, even though this seems contrary to good sense. (Pictures 164 and 165.) Leaning out this way keeps the weight on the downhill ski, and as long as it's there, the skis will edge hard into the hill and the skis cannot split apart. If the skier gets too much weight on the uphill ski, it will "climb" up the hill away from him and disrupt the traverse.

The uphill ski is given the "lead." It is advanced about six inches. The reverse position advances the uphill shoulder automatically and makes it easy to advance the uphill leg and ski. This keeps the upper ski from sliding down over the lower ski during the traverse.

The skier should look ahead across the hill, to where he is going, rather than at his feet.

The reverse that is used in the traverse is called the "countermotion" in the vocabulary of the American system; it refers to the relatively slow action of getting into the reverse position;

reverse is being used as a *position*, rather than as a fast swing of the upper body to help turn the skis. (In the latter case, it is called "counter-rotation" rather than "countermotion.")

THE STEM TURN

The next stage of the American system is the stem turn. The stem turn starts in a traverse. Then the skier moving in a traverse opens the uphill ski (or "stems" it) to assume stem position. The skier proceeds now as in the snowplow turn. The instant after the stem is made, he loads his weight onto the outside ski of the turn, and that becomes the steering ski. At the finish, when he comes back to a horizontal traverse, he closes the skis again and assumes the traverse position learned in the previous stage.

Here we see that a difference between the snowplow and the stem turn is that, in the stem, only *one* ski is brushed out to the side to form the V. In the snowplow both skis are stemmed out. Once the turns are under way, however, they look just the same.

A series of bridge sequences is used between the snowplow and the stem turn. One of the most frequently used is the practice exercise of opening and closing the uphill ski while running in a traverse. (Pictures 166 to 168.) This

original traverse

170

169

171

new traverse

172

prepares the skier for the stem turn because it teaches him to open the stem and to close it.

In the stem turn itself, the skier goes from the traverse, stems his ski, and puts his weight on the upper, outside ski of the turn. This ski steers the skier into the fall line and out of the fall line again to complete the turn. At the end, the skier slowly squeezes the inside ski together with the outside. His main weight is on the outside ski all the way through the turn. (Pictures 169 to 172.)

The stem turn allows the skier to travel across the slope more cosily, in the traverse position. (In the snowplow turn, he has to cross the slope in the stem position.) The skier simply traverses to the point where there seems to be a good place to make the turn, and he stems his uphill ski and then makes the turn.

The quicker the turn, the more the control, of course. To speed the turn, the skier will "step" hard onto the stemmed ski as he stems it; the force of the weight shift onto the ski will help the turn to start right there. Needless to say, the more weight on the outside ski, the more turning power; the S and G forces need weight to work well. The more turning power, the more rapidly the ski comes around through the fall line and into the safe, slow part of the turn coming out of the fall line to the shallow traverse.

A good skier can work into a stem turn in a few days, sometimes in a weekend. Others will have to stay with the plow for the weekend. But, in either case, the skier will have a serviceable turn for moderate slopes at the end of a couple of days, and this is the strength of the American system.

On the other hand, it should be clear by now that the skier who wants to go onward ought to go onward soon. If he spends four or five weekends stemming, he will have formed a habit that is hard to overcome when he finally tries to bring the skis together for the parallel turns.

Looking at the first stages we have just been considering, I believe an emphasis on keeping the stem turns and the plow turns short rather than long would help. This will give the skier better control.

For another thing, it would be a worthwhile experiment to see if the skier could hold off learning the traverse in favor of the sideslip (discussed in the next chapter).

It is easier to start any turn from a forward sideslip if the skier can learn to sideslip at this early stage—and I believe he can.

The main fault of the beginning stem skier is an inability to come off the traverse and start the turn downhill into the fall line. He has "traversitis," in other words.

The skier with only the stem at his disposal is going to find himself on parts of intermediate trails that are too steep for him. This is the nature of ski trails and of skiers. *If* the skier had a good forward sideslip at this point, in addition to his stem, he could avoid the difficulty of the horror spot in the trail. He could sideslip right on down. This would be a boon to other skiers who are constantly being held up at difficult sections by the stem skiers who jam the trail and cannot sideslip the steep spots.

Possibly it isn't feasible to have the average stem skier make his turns out of a sideslip, but lots of stem skiers do it, and do it beautifully, self-taught. They make great use of the forward sideslip: they go down the hill forward-and-sideways before they stem. The question is whether such skiers are unusual or whether the average skier can be taught to do this too.

Certainly every stem skier should try it for himself.

Chapter 9

THE FIRST CHRISTIE TURNS OF THE AMERICAN SYSTEM

The early christie turns and how they lead toward full parallel turns

forward side slip stops

The sideslip is the transition between the stem turns and the parallel turns of the American system.

One major requirement in the sideslip is that the skier must keep his weight on the downhill ski to keep the skis from slipping apart during the slide. If his skis split, the sideslip usually stops dead.

To get into the sideslip, the skier uses this bridge: he stands in place on a steep slope, supporting himself by his poles on the uphill and downhill sides. The trick is to make the skis go flat and to slide from the upper pole to the lower pole. The knees must move away from the slope to flatten the skis, enabling the skis to sideslip. (Pictures 176 and 177.)

Once the skier has the coordination needed to flatten the skis, he starts off in a traverse (Picture 173), hops or straightens a bit, and flattens the skis as he lands. (Picture 174.) This starts him into a "forward sideslip," in which he moves forward and down. (Picture 175.)

It is crucial for the skier to familiarize himself with the sideslip at this point in the American system. The next phases, and his own progress, depend on it.

The skier should next do the vertical sideslip. (Pictures 176 and 177.) He can further advance by doing the forward-backward sideslip, in which he first does a forward sideslip and then, by shifting his weight farther back, does a sideslip in which the tails start dropping faster, so that he moves backward (for this, the skis really have to be flat).

Another good exercise for building up sideslip is to "fit" the knee of the uphill leg over the front of the knee of the downhill leg. This "fit," in which the back of one knee is resting on the front of the other, is a constant part of skiing from this point onward in the American

original
traverse

forward sideslip

174

173

skies on edge
stay in place

flat skis sideslip

176

177

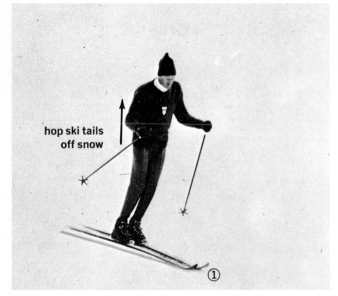

178

179

system. Note, in Picture 177, how the downhill knee seems to "carry" the uphill knee. This sets the weight on the downhill ski, where it belongs.

One further exercise to coordinate the skier is to start the forward sideslip with a hop of the skis instead of with just an up-motion. This hop motion is the more vigorous unweighting action that will be used in later turns. Thus the skier starts the downhill slide with a full hop, rather than with just an up-motion.

This work on up-motion and hop is the first point in the American system at which unweighting is brought into play. It sets the stage for the unweighting motions that follow, in the parallel turns.

The skier who can both stem and sideslip has got a fairly good set of skills. He can handle

181

182

180

ing trouble getting his turn to start down into the fall line from a traverse can often work wonders by going into a sideslip first. Once the skier is in a sideslip, where the skis are already flat and dropping, a very gentle little stem serves to start him into the turn.

THE UPHILL CHRISTIE

In the American system, the sideslip leads to the uphill christie.

The first uphill-christie exercise is practiced on the side of the hill, at a standstill. (It is reminiscent of Foeger's hop and twist exercises on the flat.)

The skier stands with skis pointing across the hill. Then he hops and turns the upper body downhill. Next, he does the same thing with an easy up-motion rather than with a hop. (Pictures 178 and 179.)

This is the first point in the American system at which the skier employs a *swift* reverse motion rather than using a slow reverse motion. In this bridge exercise to the uphill christie, the skier is actually spinning the skis with the re-

most intermediate trails, sideslipping past such moguls and down such steeps as he does not care to make turns on. The sideslip gets the skier past places that his turning skill can't dispose of. In general, the sideslip—forward-type—is a valuable and oft-neglected part of skiing, particularly for the intermediate.

The other use for the sideslip is to help the skier to turn more easily. The skier who is hav-

183

184

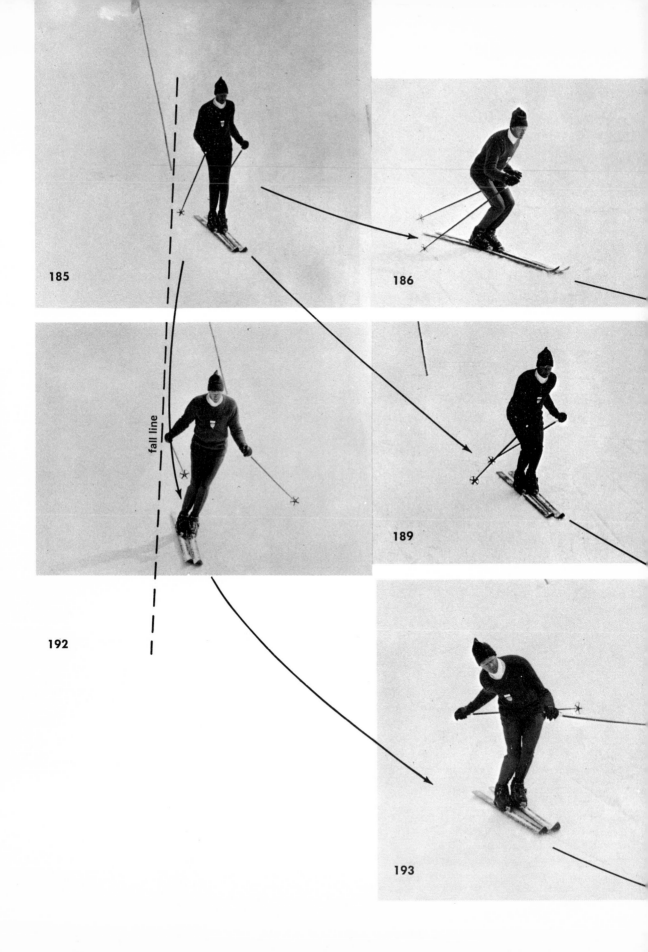

185

186

fall line

189

192

193

verse motion for the first time. In the American system, this is called "counter-rotation."

Although the ski seems to have moved at the tail only because the feet have been jumped somewhat downhill, but the result is a spin the same as a Taylor twist. If the skier jumped straight up and made the reverse motion and then came down on the same spot, it would look just like the twist. (Picture 180.)

In the uphill christie as used in the American system, the skier goes from a traverse path (Picture 181) to an up-motion (Picture 182), reverses slightly to start himself turning as he comes down with the skis fairly flat (Picture 183), and lets and S and G forces finish turning the skis. (Picture 184.)

And now a new concept is brought to bear.

The skier stops the work of the S and G forces with a "down-motion," a slow sinking with increased angulation. This sets the skis in the snow, so that they stop turning and track across the hill. (Picture 184.)

After this down-motion, the skier rises again to normal traverse position.

We have reached the point in the American system now at which a few American ski schools introduce the famous "fan" bridging sequence. (Most schools save the fan for a later time, after the next major turn, which is called the stem christie.)

In the fan sequence, the skier starts out from a given point on the slope. He starts his first run in a shallow traverse and makes an uphill christie. (Pictures 185 to 188.)

Then he makes a christie from a steeper traverse (Pictures 189 to 191), having started from the same point.

Finally, he makes a christie from the fall line. (Pictures 192 to 195.)

The ski tracks in this exercise fan out from the single starting point like ribs of a fan, giving the exercise its name. The object of the fan is to enable the skier to make longer and longer sweeping turns from a steeper and steeper angle. This sweeping parallel from the fall line is the last half of the stem-christie turn, the next turn to come.

But one American ski school, at least, makes an attempt to bypass the stem christie altogether; it maintains that, once the skiers can make the christie *from* the fall line, they can make the christie *across* the fall line. Look again at Pictures 192 to 195. They actually show a turn across the fall line rather than just "from the fall line."

Joy Lucas of PSIA has written: "If you have the pupils going down the fall line and turning their feet together, it is only a matter of minutes until they can be connecting a full parallel turn across the fall line. . . . Why split their feet again just to teach them the stem christie?"

In other words, why not go right from here to parallel?

If ski schools could bring this about, eliminating a whole turn—the stem christie—they would be making the American system a great deal more compact. As you will see in the chapter on full parallel turns, the christie *across* the fall line in the fan exercise is much like a full parallel.

BRIDGES TO STEM CHRISTIE

There is no question, however, that *some* skiers need to learn the stem christie.

The stem christie is the combination of the stem with the uphill christie. The skier uses the combination in the following manner: he stems as far as the fall line and then closes the skis to parallel out of the fall line.

It is a stable turn.

Some skiers use the "stem-christie garland" as a bridge from uphill christie to the stem christie. In this exercise, the skier starts off on a traverse, opens the uphill ski, unweights, and then closes the skis rapidly. The rapid closing motion sends both skis into an uphill christie. (Pictures 196 and 197.) A series of these is a stem-christie garland.

This procedure gives the skier practice in the up-unweighting and quick closing of the skis that occurs in the stem christie.

Other schools prefer to use the "snowplow

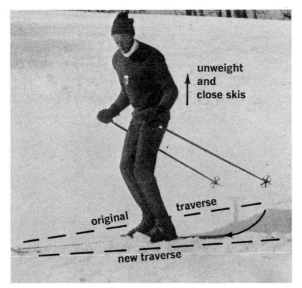

197

196

christie." This is a turn in which the skier starts out in a stem position and crouches. Then he up-unweights, closes his skis hard, and reverses with his down-motion. This gives him a fairly fast uphill christie turn out of the stem or plow position. (Pictures 198 and 199.)

The beginning stem christie starts in a stem; the stem is held until the skier turns into the fall line, and the stem is closed after that.

In the final form, the stem christie is made from the shallow traverse, starting like the stem turn. (Picture 200.) In the fall line, the skier up-unweights and brings the inside ski parallel to the outside, reversing to keep the skis turning. In this "advanced" stem christie, the skis are brought together before the fall line, so that the whole last part of the turn is a parallel turn. (Pictures 202 to 205.)

Once the skier rises rapidly and kicks the turn down into the fall line with a reverse motion, the balance is "dynamic." That is, the weight is kept on the outside ski; the skier balances over it. If the weight goes inside at this point, the skis will split, and the turn stop.

The stem carries the skier toward the fall line. From there, it is a parallel turn. The turn is stopped just as the uphill christie is stopped; at the end of the turn, when the S and G

198

199

104

201

200

202

203

204

205

forces are turning the skis, the skier simply sinks and angulates to set the edges of the skis so that they stop turning; the stem christie is then complete.

Other considerations aside, the stem christie is a good sturdy and serviceable turn. Many American skiers are in the stem-christie stage, either beginner stem christie or advanced, self-taught or school-taught. The stem christie can be used on steep slopes to maintain control in the fall line. The skier who is learning "direct parallel" cannot go on steep slopes until he learns to connect short parallel turns.

Canadian schools are also heading in this direction. The head of the Canadian schools, Ernie McCulloch, is working with a "wide-track" exercise that falls in this category.

Schools now are actively looking for short cuts to get skiers quickly into the stem christie, rather than spending much time on the stem. Once the skier is in the stem christie, the next step is parallel.

Chapter 10

ADVANCED AMERICAN TURNS

Parallel, wedeln, and split rotation and how they are related

The American-system skier next goes to the long parallel turn.

By the time he can do an advanced stem christie, the skier has a good sense of up-un-weighting before the fall line. A stem, in effect, is shoving the tail of one ski up toward the fall line. All the stem-christie skier needs to do is to replace the stem by shoving *both* skis up toward the fall line during an up-unweighting.

The traditional way of bridging to parallel is to progressively reduce the size of the stem in the stem christie, and to close the stem earlier and earlier in the turn until there is just a little "residual" stem left at the beginning of the turn.

A second and increasingly popular way of approaching parallel is to use the fan exercise. The skier starts with an uphill christie from a shallow traverse and works up to the uphill

209

210

211

206

207

208

when he springs, he turns his ski tails uphill (Picture 208) and shoves them toward the fall line, reversing to make the skis start the turn.

From here on, it is a christie across the fall line, such as the skier has already seen in the fan exercise. (Pictures 209 to 211.)

The next step up—and the bridge toward the next step (wedel)—is the "parallel with check."

We should stop here and consider what a check is.

The skier does a heel thrust and sets his edges with exaggerated angulation and reverse during a dropping motion of the whole body. This drop will bring the skier down hard on the

christie from the fall line. Finally, he does an uphill christie *across* the fall line. This is not so very far from the full parallel turn.

The full parallel first done by the skier in the American system is called "parallel without check."

The skier starts on a traverse. (Picture 206.) Then he goes into a crouch (Picture 207, much as he does for the uphill christie, except that

214

213

212

217

218

219

220

edges and cause a sudden stop or slowing down. This is a check. It "sets" the skis.

To make a parallel with check, the skier simply goes from a traverse (Picture 212) to a check (Picture 213), and then uses an up-motion to start the turn (Picture 214) down the hill. It is like an ordinary parallel from there on.

The parallel with check is the first form in which the American-system skier really uses his poles. The parallel with check is designed to

take the skier onto steeper slopes with his long parallel turn. He will not only have to brake harder (by means of a check) to keep his speed down; he will have to unweight more quickly and positively, using the "set" position as a stable take-off platform.

The most generally used bridge to parallel with check is the "check hop garland." This is a form of practice for the very beginning part of the turn.

The skier goes on a traverse, makes a short heel thrust, sets the skis as in a check, sets the pole in the snow on the down-motion, and then hops the tails a bit up the hill, as if starting down into the turn. However, he does not make the turn. He lets the tails of the skis land and slide back to the traverse path they had before.

The skier makes a row of these "check hops" to make the check hop garland.

When the skier can make several check hops in a row without any trouble, he is ready for the "parallel with check."

PARALLEL WITH CHECK

The parallel with check goes as follows: the skier starts from his traverse, makes the check, and uses this solid footing as a platform from which to take off on his parallel turn—up-unweighting with the hop or up-motion, using the pole, reversing to get the initial turn of the skis down the hill toward the fall line—and from there it is like the parallel without check (Pictures 215 to 221) done previously.

It is very important that the skier should not use the pole wrongly here. The pole has to be used to unweight, so that it thrusts the skier

221

222

upward. It should not be used to "hook" the skier into the turn. It is planted close to the skis and the skier "rides over" the handle of the pole, using the reverse motion not leverage from the pole to swing the skis into the turn.

This is a great turn for steep slopes. The check and hop kill the skier's speed and make it easy to turn on a small spot.

223

224

planting pole

The only thing missing now for control in steep slopes is the short turn. And that comes next, with wedel.

WEDEL TURNS

There has been some confusion between short parallel and wedel. Technically, wedel is a series of short parallels without any connecting traverses. But there is such a thing as a short parallel turn by itself. Each short parallel, individually, can be called a wedel turn. But the word "wedel" by itself means a series of these turns.

Wedel is the last of the final forms in the

225

American system. There are various wedels, from the very flat "schmieren," with no edge set, to normal wedel with some edging, to the hard-edged carved wedel and on to the "hop wedel" for very steep slopes.

Essentially the flat-ski wedel is a way of practice, or a bridge to the carved wedel and hop wedel used on steep slopes. The wedel on a moderate slope is wonderful fun and a marvelous rhythm exercise, but the really useful wedels are the steep-slope wedels, where the short radius of the turn and the hard braking of the edge-work serve as a way to keep the skier's speed under good control.

To keep the turns short, each turn is cut off and a new turn started before the skis reach a shallow traverse. At the edge-set that ends the turn, the skis are usually still in a fairly steep diagonal, as in Picture 228. The skier in the picture is about to start a new wedel turn.

Since there is so short a distance between turns, and since the pole is used to help un-weighting, the pole action has to be fast. As soon as the skier has placed one pole and ridden over it to begin one turn, the other pole must be brought forward to be planted for the next turn.

BRIDGES TO WEDEL

One good bridge to wedel is the wedel pole exercise. The skier goes down the fall line of

228

up motion

226

227

a gentle slope and places first one pole and then the next, "walking" the poles down the hill. He passes the pole in each case without attempting to use it for unweighting. (Picture 222.)

Next, while doing the same thing, he uses the pole at each plant to make an up-motion, letting the tails of the skis come down straight. (Picture 223.)

Next, he again does the same thing, except that he makes a heel thrust to the side away

fall line

from the pole when he comes down. (Pictures 224 and 225.)

The sequence is "plant, hop, and heel thrust."

At the end of the heel thrust, he plants the pole for the next hop, as in Picture 226.

The skier first concentrates on making one wedel turn at a time and then, as he goes toward the "continuous turning" of wedel, he starts putting the turns closer together.

To arrive at wedel, the skier simply reduces the hop motion and makes it smooth and quick, a little up-motion, so that the tails of the skis do not leave the snow. (Picture 227.) Then he connects one turn to the next, so that as soon as he comes out of one turn, he is going into another one.

When he gets the real feel of it, the skier will be thinking of it as a number of connected heel thrusts, with the thrust being made almost straight out to the sides from the fall line. In Picture 228, the skier is thrusting across the fall line.

The reason for getting the turns so closely connected is that short turns and continuous turning are the best defense against steepness. There is every reason to eliminate traverses between turns on a steep hill, if you want to control your descent properly. The skier may have to make a turn every half-second or so on the steepest part if he really wants to keep his speed down.

Wedel served as a trademark for the whole Austrian system when the system was first introduced over here. Wedel, however, is only the final turn of the Austrian system, not the whole of it.

WIDE TRACK

There is a useful sequence to improve wedel that is being used by Ernie McCulloch. It is called "wide-track." As used at McCulloch's school at Mont Tremblant, Quebec, it has a variety of applications. It can get the stem-christie skier into short parallel turns. It can help the skier who can only make the long

parallel go into short parallel, and it can give a skier the rhythm for wedel.

However it is used, it is one of the new ideas in skiing.

Exercises that teach the skier to "face downhill" at the beginning and that teach short turns to begin with have a great future.

At the McCulloch school, the bridge sequence has three parts: wide track, narrow track, and parallel.

To start, the skier moves down the hill in a snowplow. Then he picks up the left ski, so that the weight is entirely on the right. Now he jumps both skis toward the side of the weighted (right) ski. He lands with the skis fairly far apart.

In effect, this is a short, crude hop-wedel: poles are used to help the jump. When the skier jumps left, the right pole pushes him over there, and so on. (Pictures 229 to 232.)

In the second stage, narrow-track wedel, the skis are brought closer together, to within six inches or so. The skis are not stemmed as much. In the last stage, parallel hop wedel, the skis are together and there is no stem at all. Adding positive heel thrust to this gives a standard hop wedel. The skier reduces this hop to up-motion for normal wedel.

If he wants long turns, he can start carving the skis to get smooth parallel christies across the fall line.

The inspiration for the wide-track–narrow-track exercise comes from an analysis of movie-camera studies of children teaching themselves to ski. They will stem an uphill ski, put some weight on it, crouch a bit, and then jump both ski tails to the uphill side. This starts off a short slewed turn. As a learning device, this has turned into a very successful exercise.

I have always maintained that there is much to learn from self-taught skiers. They naturally tend to simplify as much as possible, and they often come up with sound procedures. They naturally tend to favor the short turn, which gives them lots of control. This makes sense. The slewed wedel turn is a natural development of the wide-track–narrow-track exercise above.

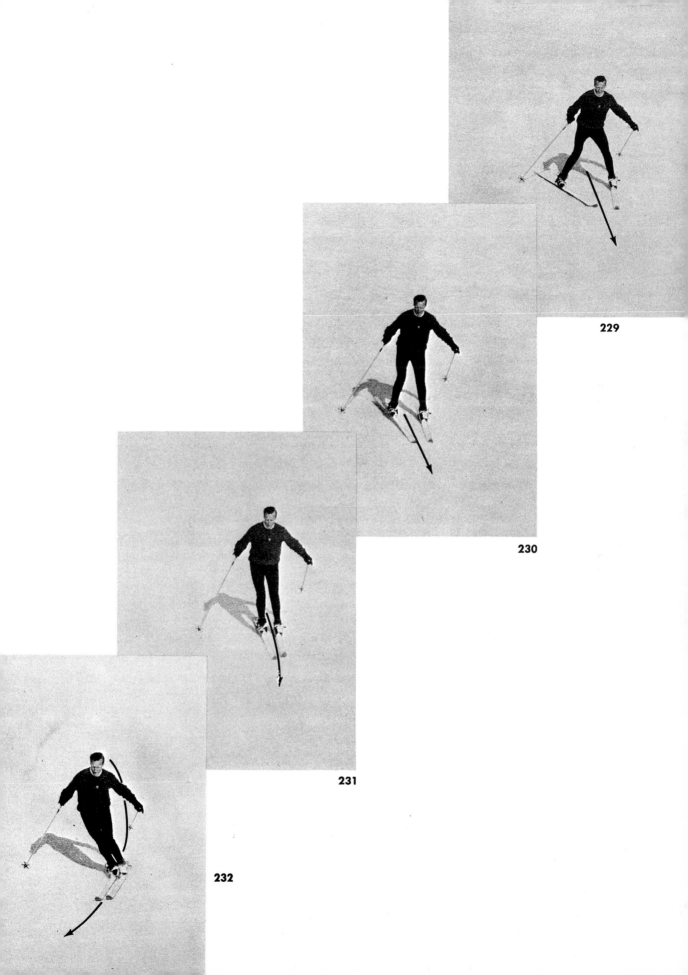

229

230

231

232

234

233

Probably this exercise, coupled with other well-worked-out bridging sequences, will eventually be widely used to teach parallel right from the snowplow stage, particularly to talented skiers. The Austrians under Kruckenhauser are now introducing this under the name *"offener schwung,"* or open swing.

235

Canadian skier down-unweights to continue his parallel turns.

236

The act of hopping the tails back and forth as in the wide-track exercise involves reverse power, just as heel thrust does. In the wide-track–narrow-track exercise the skis may be lifted clear of the snow. It is obvious that middle-body muscles are turning the skis; even if the tips are left on the snow, the snow does not turn the skis. The body does.

When it comes to wedel, there are very small differences in the four major systems, Austrian, French, American, and Canadian. The down-motion and the up-motion stressed in one system or another at earlier stages blend into the up-down bobbing movement of the wedel. Both up-unweighting and down-unweighting, consecutively used, figure in the wedel.

THE CANADIAN SYSTEM

In the long parallel turns, however, there is a difference. The long parallel of the American uses an up-unweighting up-motion, where the Canadian uses a down-motion. The Canadian schools' reverse-motion is definitely more subdued. (Pictures 233 to 236.) The shoulders are held more "square" (not reversed as much) through the turn.

This, however, is the major difference in the Canadian schools in the United States. The Canadian Ski Instructors Alliance, headed by McCulloch, has instructors very much on a par with those of the American system, and there are no real differences (other than usual differences in "method") between the classes in the Canadian and the United States systems.

THE FRENCH SYSTEM

In the French parallel, which is taught in only one or two schools in the United States, there is a great difference. The French use a definite rotation rather than a reverse to start the long parallel turn.

The question arises whether the French keep some of their rotation movement in short parallel turns, i.e., when they wedel. The answer is they

reversing to finish first turn

237

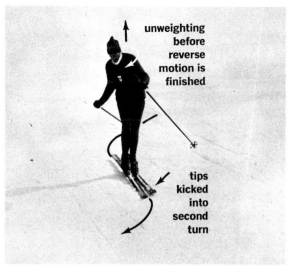

unweighting before reverse motion is finished

tips kicked into second turn

238

new reverse motion finishes second turn

239

240

241

long parallel
turn finished by S and G forces   242

do. This procedure can blend with the normal United States-Austrian wedel and be helpful. Many good skiers from all systems use a little rotation to smooth up their wedel and make it more powerful. It's "split-rotation wedel."

When the wedel turn is finished in a heel thrust, as all good wedel turns should be, the reversing motion that ends the heel thrust *can* be carried over into the next turn as a rotation movement *into* that turn.

It works this way.

The skier who has finished his turn with an energetic reverse motion can do one of two things. He can absorb all this energy by setting his edges hard and *stopping* the reverse motion. Or he can start unweighting *before* the reverse motion is completely finished. In this case the very last part of the reverse motion tends to *knock* the tips of the skis into the next turn as the reverse motion is slowed down and comes to a stop. This effect has been given various names —"tip pull," "pre-rotation," "split rotation," "anticipation." Whatever it is called, it works.

USING SPLIT ROTATION

The skier who wants to use split rotation times his reverse so that he is unweighting for his next turn as he blocks or ends the reverse motion of his last turn. (Picture 238.) This blocking of the reverse motion kicks the skis into the next turn. (Picture 239.)

Split rotation can also be made to work in the long parallel. The skier comes up with his unweighting motion and makes a slight rotation of the upper body toward the new turn. He blocks the motion abruptly. (Picture 241.) The tips twist slightly into the new turn and the skier then reverses, his upper body twisting (Picture 242) to finish it off. Split rotation is a very efficient way to start a parallel turn, and many expert skiers use it.

Some of the split-rotation action in the long turn results from Foeger's "counter-comma position." (Figure B in picture 243.) The move into the counter-comma kicks the tips of the

rotation
toward
the turn
(move into
counter-comma)

A

B

traversing

beginning
of
reverse

movement
away
from
turn

C

D

E

traverse

exaggerated rotation
toward turn
kicks tip into turn

244

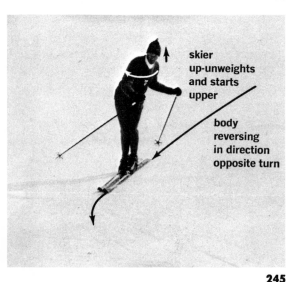

skier
up-unweights
and starts
upper

body
reversing
in direction
opposite turn

245

finish of
reverse
motion in
mambo turn

246

skis into the turn just a bit. The reversing motion begins, sending the skier into the "regular" comma position in which he finishes the turn.

The little rotation motion at the beginning of the split-rotation turn sets the body up so that it gets the longest possible reverse swing. The split-rotation movement, then, not only kicks the skis into the turn but sets up a more powerful reverse motion.

Some degree of split rotation can also be seen in the American-system parallel turn (see the sequence at the beginning of this chapter).

MAMBO

This brings us to mambo, an exaggeration of split rotation. The skier who wants to mambo simply does the split rotation and holds off blocking the initial rotation as long as he can.

The skier who mambos makes a full rotation of the upper body to start with and carries his lead arm over to the far side of his skis, as far as he can. Then, because the middle muscles can't stretch any farther (Picture 244), the rotation is blocked or slowed down and the skis are pulled into the turn, provided the skier has the skis flat at that moment so that they don't offer much resistance.

The skier now starts into a full reverse, which keeps the skis moving in the same direction (a rotation to the right and a reverse to the left both tend to move the skis to the right). As you can see in Picture 245, the reverse finished the turn for the skier.

When his reverse ends, it has shot the skis around to the new traverse. (Picture 246.)

The skier continues his reverse, but it now becomes a rotation into the next turn, because it is starting to be slowed down or blocked willy-nilly in the middle muscles, which are beginning to be stretched to the limit. And so it goes, back and forth, with the upper body leading the skis into each turn.

Mambo is lots of fun. It looks good, and it is a way of learning split rotation. But, in itself, it is more of an exercise than a useful turn.

Chapter 11

SLOPE SAVVY

The problems of terrain and what the skier can do about them

The skier seldom has ideal conditions. In addition to the challenge of the technique, there is the challenge of the terrain and the kind of snow.

One challenge is steepness. Most trails designated "intermediate" with regard to the average slope also have a few expert spots. The same is true with most beginner's trails: they have intermediate spots in them somewhere.

And so the challenge of steepness must be met early in every skier's life.

This doesn't mean that the skier should go out of his way to find challenge. There is nothing so detrimental to learning as a slope too steep to handle. Keep to the moderate slope at the beginning of the day if you are trying to learn some technique. You then can concentrate on form rather than on the slope. I have watched skiers fume because bad weather confined them to the "easy" slopes. But while they were confined to the easy slopes, they worked out bugs in their skiing. They finally had time to think about their faults.

Besides steepness, there is challenge of ice (or boiler plate), the challenge of close-set bumps (moguls), and the challenge of surplus snow (powder or heavy, loose snow).

We'll deal with the snow problem in the next chapter. Here we'll take up steepness and moguls.

Steepness is, first of all, a psychological hazard. The skier tends to lean in *toward* the hill on a steep slope rather than increase his lean *away* from the hill. The skier must, instead, lean out over the downhill ski, which is the safe ski.

The true steepness problem is in starting his turn down the hill into the fall line. If the skier finds himself "stuck," he can often get out simply by going into a vertical or (preferably) a forward sideslip and then making the turn. The very fact that the skis are moving down the hill sideways makes the turn down the hill easier, both psychologically and as a matter of engineering forces.

STEEP STEM TURNS

The stem skier must, to get the turn started, get his weight onto the uphill ski, which is the ski he is starting to stem. It will help him if he flattens the downhill ski as he starts the stem, thus slipping down as he stems. Then only very little pressure on the uphill ski will be needed to start the turn into the fall line. Hard edging of the downhill ski to keep the ski from slipping also makes it very hard to turn that ski into the fall line. The skier should let the downhill ski slip and *then* make the turn.

The over-edging of the downhill ski is often the cause of the "refusal" of the skis to go into a downhill turn on steep terrain.

The skier must not over-edge the uphill ski, either. If he does, the ski will tend to "track" rather than turn. He should start the edging with a small angle to the snow and increase it with a slow inward bend of the ankle and the uphill knee as the turn starts. Then, once in the fall line, the skier can edge very positively to give braking power.

It goes without saying that the stem skier has the special problem of shortening his turn on steep slopes. The shorter the turn, the slower the speed at the end of the turn.

The stem skier can shorten his turn in two ways. First he should make the move onto the stemmed ski a fast one, first practicing on moderate terrain. The weight should be thrust onto the stemmed ski in one swift "step." Springing out onto the stemmed ski solidly as he stems it is the answer. If this ski is properly edged (not too much), the ski will be pushed into the turn by the skier's momentum. The turn will start fast, coming into the fall line quickly and out again before the skier has picked up much speed.

Once the ski is well started, he must *keep* the weight on that ski. A lot of skiers who *think* they have the weight out there don't. They lean in toward the hill and fall inward. The skier who has enough weight on the outside ski should be able to pick the inside ski *completely* off the snow at the end of the turn. He should try this as a "stem-improvement exercise," picking the ski up toward the end of the turn and holding it up. He will see that the extra weight he gets on the outside ski shortens the turn.

This exercise and the wide-track wedel exercise of the last chapter are the two best weight-shifting exercises for the stem skier who wants to shorten his turns and keep his speed down.

The other secret of good stem skiing on steeper slopes is to connect the turns.

CONNECTING STEM TURNS

The best way to connect the turns is to cut each turn short, so that the skier doesn't go all the way to a *shallow* traverse before starting the next turn down into the fall line again. If he is in a rather steep traverse, it will be much easier to start a turn. He has a greater force of gravity working for him. Gravity is a great help in starting a turn. Granted, the skier won't slow down quite so much at the end of each turn as he will if he goes to a shallow traverse; yet it is tactically better to make three or four connected turns at medium speed than to make one turn to a shallow traverse, stop, and then painfully start up again.

It is best to try to cut each turn short and start the next one early. If the skier becomes stuck, he should try to stay in a steep traverse by sideslipping rather than go all the way around to a shallow traverse.

Above all, the stem skier should stay off continuously steep slopes. It is better to get to parallel by learning on moderate slopes. *Then* one can go to the steeper stuff.

PARALLEL ON STEEP SLOPES

A parallel skier on steep slopes must—for control—unweight strongly and get the skis turning quickly to get a short, hard-breaking turn. He shouldn't "jump the skis around." The skier who jumps the skis halfway around is not solving the problem. This kind of jump turn is too exhausting and acrobatic. The right way is to unweight fast, turn the skis a few degrees and then slide with full weight on the skis as they go through the fall line. Jump-turning the skis through the fall line makes for a hard landing and a loss of balance. The very best skiers keep their skis in the snow as much as possible, even during the unweighting. They flatten the skis to connect turns rather than unweighting completely, letting the skis brush through the snow, shoving them through the snow to the side for the start of a turn. This gives a smoother start.

The skis ought to be quite flat when the skier "lands" on them to go into the sliding part of the turn. If the skis are too much on edge, they will "track" instead of turning as the skier comes down from his unweighting. This means that the turn will stop right there, with the skier headed straight down the fall line—exactly what he is trying to prevent.

It helps also if the skier lands "softly," with plenty of knee action as he lands. This will keep the skis from being pushed too far into the snow surface, where they might prevent turning.

The problem of the landing, however, is not so prevalent as the problem of the take-off. Nine times out of ten, when the skis refuse to go through with a parallel turn on a slope, steep or not, the skier hasn't unweighted *enough*.

The lack of proper unweighting makes the skis balk in the transition between turns because there is still too much friction under them for the skier's body motion to break them into the turn. If the skier finds his skis refusing the turn, he should start exaggerating his up-motion. The problem will usually clear up right away.

The parallel skier has several other weapons when it comes to turning on a steep slope.

The first is the check. The purpose of the American-system "parallel with check" is to teach this little trick. A good hard check before each turn will work wonders on a steep slope. The skier thrusts hard, checking his speed, and makes a good solid "platform" from which to take off for the unweighting and reverse into the next turn.

If the check and unweighting are timed right, he receives an assist from the "rebound" of the ski. The ski tends to bend into a bow during the check. It immediately springs back, and if the skier springs with it, he gets a boost. The skier who learns to work with his skis this way has a good thing going for him. Springing with the ski saves a lot of work, and the expert skier prefers a good stiff ski for packed-snow conditions.

One good way to prepare for a steep trail is

to spend twenty minutes on an easy trail practicing "check hop garlands" and getting the timing right so that you spring with the ski.

It is, of course, highly desirable to make short parallel turns to control speed in steep terrain.

SHORTENING THE PARALLEL TURN

The parallel skier can shorten his turn in several ways. The first is to apply explosive reverse action to power the skis as far around as he can before letting the S and G forces take over. He should think of turning the skis rather than the shoulders; the shoulders take care of themselves.

A second way is to practice a little split rotation on the steep slope. (Picture 247.) This will set up a position for a powerful reverse to continue the turn. But, split rotation should not be overdone. About six inches of movement of the outside shoulder in the direction of the turn as the skier starts to come up for the unweighting is enough. The blocking of the shoulder movement should occur as the skier becomes weightless. Then, of course, the skier starts to reverse good and hard, and the skis keep turning in the direction in which they were started.

Another little trick on steep slopes can be used anywhere. It is to get the weight on the outside ski early in the parallel turn. The skier does not wait for the ski to reach the fall line: he puts his weight on it almost immediately by proper use of the pole. (Picture 248.) The faster he puts his weight on the uphill ski, the sooner it starts to act as a braking force. The ski, while it is unweighted, does not act as a braking force at all. "Weight on the uphill ski" may sound contrary, but it is merely a case of weight on the outside ski of the coming turn, which is standard practice. By getting onto that ski *early*, the skier keeps the unweighting period very short and lengthens the braking period.

The turn itself, of course, has to be short. Rather than hopping high, he down-unweights. The skier who really controls his skis is thrusting

247. *Skier coming down Exhibition Run in Sun Valley is using split rotation to start his turn. Note the forward sweep of the left arm as he starts to unweight.*

248. *Junior Bounous getting his weight onto the uphill ski preparatory to making a downhill turn.*

the skis out to one side, letting them turn out there as he drops down on them and then thrusting them out to the other side. The skis stay in the snow, the skier's body doesn't rise, and there is always *some* pressure on the skis to keep them brushing the snow. This procedure provides a much smoother series of turns than the normal up-motion or hop wedel.

Cutting each turn off also creates short parallels. Too many skiers work hard at finishing each turn, edging around to the shallow traverse each time. They could be going down the hill with half the work, if they cut the turns off short, putting in more and easier turns per foot of trail.

CONNECTING TURNS

The skier should always plan to make his last turn so that he ends up facing the middle of the trail. Many skiers, unfortunately, make a turn, go into a traverse, and then come to a dead stop at the edge of the trail, facing the woods. It is much better for the skier to make a last turn *away* from the edge and *then* stop, so that he faces the middle. Then he is in a good position to start his next turn from a standstill: he has the whole width of the trail in front of him. The skier who always stops facing the middle of the trail may find that there don't

249

250

253

254

251

252

255

have to be any last turns. Instead of stopping, he can go on making turns.

But suppose you *have* skied yourself into a corner. You are at a standstill facing the woods. This is where the "standing turns" come in. Basically, there are two turns that can be done at a standstill, enabling you to turn around and face the trail again. One is the kick turn, an exquisite maneuver. The more common one for beginning skiers is the gambit of "walking the ski tails uphill." Both turns should be practiced on the flat, of course.

WALKING TAILS UPHILL

To walk the tails uphill, the skier firmly plants both poles below him in the snow. The skis are in a horizontal position, well-edged to keep the skier from sideslipping. The poles should be planted far enough away so that the skier can lean on them, straighten both elbows, and put his full weight on the poles. Poles should be about three or four feet apart in the snow.

First, the skier moves the tail of the uphill ski two feet or so farther up the hill, leaving the tip where it is. This puts him in a stem position. Then he moves the lower ski up, parallel with the upper ski. He is now facing somewhat down the hill, leaning his weight hard on the poles. This sounds like a tall order, but if the skier locks his elbows by keeping his arms straight, he will be able to do it nicely. He now keeps on stepping the skis around in a half-circle until he is facing into the trail. At the very worst, if he should let go, he is on his way down the hill and can make a turn to face the middle of the trail.

In the kick turn, the skier places both poles ahead of him and leans forward on them, putting all the weight on the upper ski, which has to be edged well into the hill. (Pictures 249 and 250.) Then he kicks the tip of the downhill ski into the air, sets the tail of that ski into the snow by his other ski tip (Picture 251), and lets the ski fall over into the opposite track. (Picture 252.) The skier now has one ski facing in each direction. (Picture 253.) The trick is to stay relaxed, and take one's time. Once the first ski is down, the skier can lean forward onto that ski (Picture 254) and then, picking up the remaining ski, swing it around parallel to the first so that both skis now face into the trail. (Picture 255.)

The kick turn used to be taught to skiers on the first day or so on the slope, but wisdom has prevailed and it is now taught later, when the skier is more relaxed about his situation. The relaxation of the leg muscles is the key.

A third alternative, when the skier is standing face to face with unskiable terrain, is to start a vertical sideslip, then move the weight forward to force the tips to drop first and simultaneously stem the uphill ski. This will turn the skier out of the predicament. This "sideslip and stem" can be accomplished in a rather confined space. Three or four feet of clearance between the skier and the "edge" is enough. If he doesn't have the clearance, he can always back up until he does.

Best of all, one shouldn't get into this situation in the first place.

MOGUL PROBLEMS

So much for the problems on steep hills. Now we consider moguls.

The mogul is a modern phenomenon, brought about by the fact that skiers make fairly short turns on steep slopes. A mogul is a man-made mound; it grows because skiers tend to follow in each other's short turns down the hill. The snow gets pushed into a pile in the center of the turns. Other skiers, in going over the piles, pack them into polished little mounds—or big mounds if the slope is steep enough. On easy slopes there is no tendency to make short turns, and so there are no moguls. You can take an aerial photograph of a ski area and pinpoint the steep slopes simply by noticing where the moguls show up.

Moguls cost ski areas a lot of money. Most skiers don't like them. Ski-area managers use men and machines to break moguls up and smooth them off, hoping to please the skiers. The skiers build up the moguls again.

One way out of this vicious circle is to persuade skiers to like moguls. Actually, moguls can be a lot of fun.

There are two ways of skiing them: slow and steady, over the tops, for one. Fast and sneaky around the bottoms is the other.

If one is a stem skier, one should try the high road. It helps if a mogul is nicely rounded on top, and many of them are. Then the skier approaches the mogul and skis up onto it. He stems as he reaches the top, and turns over the brim of the mogul, sideslipping the downhill face of it. Turning over a bump this way is easy. The tip and tail of the ski are out of the snow so the ski turns without much effort.

Once the skier comes off a mogul, sideslipping safely and slowly down the far face of it, he must now turn again on the next mogul if possible. The art is to turn on almost every mogul to keep one's speed low.

The low road is a more sophisticated mogul method and more beloved by the better skier.

It is a question of checking on the uphill face of the mogul or the side of the mogul and mak-

256. *Pepi Gramshammer, a world champion, formerly from Austria and now at Vail, does a pre-jump over a lip. He is shown extending his legs to touch down again at the end of the pre-jump. The maneuver meant that he avoided being tossed into the air over the lip of the drop-off in the background.*

ing a hard turn to the next mogul. The skier checks on the side or uphill face of this next mogul and goes on. It is a real chess game. A highly skilled practitioner of the low-road method is called a "river runner" and his action, "river-running." In effect, the skier is running through the "rivers" between the moguls and mostly avoiding the tops.

The skier who can do this at a good speed is in line for his expert skier's merit badge. For one thing, the skier cannot make his turns at will, as on a smoother slope. He has to adjust his turns to the radius of the moguls. This means starting at the right time; putting just enough edge in so that the ski carves onto and off the mogul again, coming to a heel thrust check very quickly so that he kills his speed (most of the "rivers" between the moguls lie right in the fall line) before carving onto the side of the next one. If he should make his turn too short, the tails of his skis will swing against a mogul and that will throw him off balance.

The skier still has to maintain a certain rhythm in his turns. It is like dancing. He fits his rhythm to the rhythm of the moguls, and it can be a great waltz.

Moguls often *do* have a rhythm to them, since they were originally formed by the turns of skiers. Sometimes you get an out-of-rhythm mogul, and then you have to go straight over it.

TAKING MOGULS STRAIGHT

The problem of going straight over a mogul is like the problem of handling any bump. The proper way is for the skier to "pull up" or lift his skis as he crosses the mogul, and then press his skis down on the down side of the mogul; this enables him to set them quickly into a turn; he has by now presumably gained considerable headway. A few feet of straight running on a steep hill translates into speed almost as fast as that of a man in a free fall.

The wrong way to go over a mogul is to ride over it stiff-legged. This causes the mogul to lift the skier into the air. The aerial leap can be spectacular, of course, if the skier can handle the problems that this creates. The non-kannonen skier knows his limits and "lifts" the skis over. His head hardly rises at all as he passes over the mogul. His legs draw up neatly under him and then press down again as he feels the mogul dropping away on the far side. "Lift and press" is the safe sequence.

Any sudden dip in the slope can be handled by the same technique. The skier treats the far side of the dip as the face of a bump and lifts his skis out of the dip, departing unscathed.

Lastly, this technique can be used to handle a real drop-off. The skier would rather keep his skis on the snow than go sailing off the top of the drop. He simply pulls his skis up a bit just before he gets to the lip of the drop. (The name of the maneuver is "pre-jump.") The skier is already dropping as he goes over the lip. As he passes the lip, he presses his skis into the snow, hard, and maintains contact with it as it drops away under him. As long as he is in contact with the snow, he can make turns and control himself.

This does it for steeps and bumps.

Chapter 12

MORE SLOPE SAVVY—WESTERN SKIING

The inside story on ice—too little snow; the other extreme—too much snow

A friend of mine who had been an Easterner once skied Aspen with me. As we finished off a trail, his skis struck ice with a nasty sound. He turned around and said, "What was that? We never hear that sound out here!" Ice, in other words, is mainly an Eastern problem. The advice below is dedicated to the two-thirds of the ski population that lives in the East.

There is only one solution to real "blue ice." That is to keep a pair of "blue-ice skis." A ski-school head I know keeps a pair of skis that he takes out four or five times a year, when the slopes go to sheet ice. (This is what is meant by "blue ice.") At the end of the year, he trades them for a new pair. The edges of his "blue-ice skis" never see much use, and so, when they are used, they cut into the ice like knives. There is nothing like new edges for ice. The second-best thing is to resharpen the edges on Old Faithfuls, your only pair of skis. However, re-sharpened edges don't cut quite like new ones. But a sharp edge *is* the single best anti-ice device. The sides of the edge should form a square, not a round, corner.

Fortunately, most ice on the slopes is not pure and blue; it is patchy, white ice. The best thing the skier can do with a small ice patch is to run straight over it without making turns.

He should make his turn on the far side. He must not be proud: he should put about six inches between the skis for stability, run over it parallel, and bend both knees just slightly inward to turn the skis up on their inside edges. This keeps the skis from "wandering" over the ice as the skier runs across it.

(Incidentally, any time a skier does have trouble with skis wandering during a schuss (straight run), ice or not, he can straighten them out by putting them on the inside edges. If his skis wander all the time, they may be warped or worn out.)

SIDESLIPPING AND TURNING

If the skier doesn't want to build up the extra speed, it is perfectly possible to sideslip ice rather than schuss it. The skier has to "go" with the lower ski, with no hesitation. The sideslip will be a fast one. He must not try to make a stop check in the middle of the patch or he'll lose everything. He has to be satisfied that he is going across this ice as slowly as is possible. Sideways speed may seem fast, but it really is not. It is just a question of getting used to the idea of sideways speed. The skier keeps the skis flat and stands relaxed, very straight and balanced over them; he will arrive at the other side with as good control as he could expect, given the size of the ice patch.

If a skier *has* to make turns on ice, he should use very little edging. The skier who edges hard on ice is going to get "chatter" in his skis. These are very unsettling rapid vibrations that make the skis hard to control. Hard edging may also cause the skis to "track" rather than turn. On ice, the skier should exaggerate the comma from the knee and waist, however. Getting more weight on the outside ski is a lifesaver here.

A more common condition is near-ice, or "boiler plate," a condition that often persists on a whole mountain. If the skier has good edges, he can turn fairly well on moderate boiler-plate slopes. But, again, he has to under-edge and not try to make too many hard turns. Nice, easy, rounded turns, plenty of weight on the outside ski are called for. If he gets into difficulties, he should sideslip rather than stop, at least for the first few feet. If he *has* to stop fast, he can do it, but he has to make a very muscular and exaggerated stop turn, with a comma that almost bends him double. Most skiers don't have too many stops like that in them on a given day.

Boiler-plate turns are ones where I like to forget parallel and use stem christies, just for the sake of keeping my edges in harder contact with the slope at all times.

There usually are alleviating circumstances with boiler plate. The first is that the ski-area manager may take pity and send up a few snow tractors to break up the boiler plate on the intermediate slopes. In this case, one should ski those. Or there may be trails that face south on the slope. If this is so, and there is a bit of sun, these trails will be considerably more hospitable, for they soften slightly. If one trail is much more heavily used than the others, this slope will be cut up enough after a while to become passable skiing for all.

But the usual alleviation is the presence of patches of loose snow, particularly at the sides of the trail. In this case, the skier pilots from one of these to the other, making his turn as soon as he hits a patch. This may sound simple, but there is great art to it. Nothing is so stirring to an Eastern skier as seeing a real pro go down a slope of boiler plate touching bits of loose snow that no one else has spotted, skiing as smoothly as if he were in ankle-deep powder. A skier who can spot these patches and string them together in a series of turns is a fine slope-strategist.

Some of the time it isn't even that hard. The sides of the trails often are swimming with snow. The skier who can cut his turns short and keep connecting them has no real problem. He can stay right in the ribbon of snow.

Even a stem skier can do this. Unfortunately, most stem skiers don't. They know how to make the full stem turn from shallow traverse to shallow traverse, and that is all they know. They ski out in the middle, fighting boiler plate like a Class D farm-team rookie swinging at curves.

I would venture to say that a snowplow skier, using something like Ernie McCulloch's wide-track exercise, *could* stay along the sides using short connected turns, if he had been shown how to do it.

BOOTS AND ICE

Lastly, boots can have an effect on skiing boiler plate. A boot with a good stiff "upper" will make skiing icy trails very much easier than a soft boot with worn-out leather around the ankles. And when icy conditions prevail, this is the time for the skier to lace or buckle the boot as tight as he can and still maintain circulation in his feet.

That is about the whole story on ice and boiler plate: good edges, good boots, good short turns along the snowy sides, good judgment in picking trails that may be less icy, and, best of all, good humor. You will ski better if you don't get mad at the slope. If all skiing were good, then good skiing would be a bore.

DEEP-SNOW CHALLENGES: POWDER

This brings us to the question of "surplus snow."

The first kind of surplus-snow condition is the best: powder. Some Eastern areas boast that they have "heavy powder" on a given day, but what they have is *not* powder. It is just heavy new snow. Powder is light, airy and *dry*, by definition.

Powder is delightful. A covering of two inches over hard-packed snow turns average skiing into great skiing. Four inches is heaven. But after that, the skier has to vary his technique a bit. By the time there is a foot of powder, skiing is almost another sport altogether.

The skier going through a foot of new powder will have sensations unlike anything on hard-pack. In the first place, the powder will tend to snatch his inside ski away and cause it to "hook" to the inside. In the second place, it makes the turn down into the fall line very much harder, and the turn out of the fall line somewhat easier, so that skiers not used to powder find themselves continually running out to the side in a shallow traverse, unable to make a decent turn back into the fall line again.

The Western skiers have worked out a whole technique for handling powder, which is quite different from the way Eastern skiers ski. In the first place, the Westerner skis much squarer over the skis. There is very little reversing or angulation in the turn, in other words. The Western skiers tend rather to make a short rotation to start the turn and then ride a long carved turn with the whole body leaning inward in a diagonal direction. Long before they reach the traverse line, they bounce up quite high, rotate slightly, lean inward to the other side, and ride out a new turn. The whole thing looks exasperatingly easy. But it is an entire technique in itself.

The principles underlying the Western style are as follows.

In the first place, the skis must be pretty evenly weighted in deep powder. The reason

257. *The square stance of the powder skier is illustrated here by the skier doing a traverse in powder at Sun Valley. The "square" stance with shoulders at right angles to the skis is more like the Canadian style of skiing, or the French. Both tend to have a squarer traverse than the Austrian or American styles.*

that the Easterner finds his inside ski being snatched away is that the snow grabs whichever ski has less weight on it and tends to twist it away. Not only do the skis have to be evenly weighted but the legs have to be actively *squeezed* together in the parallel turn, to keep the snow from piling in between the legs and splitting the skis.

Angulation would tend to put the weight on the outside ski, and this disrupts the even weighting. A "square" upright style weights the skis evenly.

A little rotation seems to work better in starting the turn, because it pulls the tips gently into the turn, allowing the skier to keep his square stance with less disturbance—and the square stance is the key to the style. The Western skier uses just a little bit of reverse toward the end of the turn—but not enough to endanger the delicate balance. It is for this reason that the Western skiers have always been advocates of split rotation: it works so well in powder.

258. *The powder skier typically edges by leaning the whole body toward the inside of the turn, as Nick Fiore is doing here at Badger Pass. The standard reverse skier would be in a comma here, "looking downhill."*

259. *The danger of leaning toward the center of the turn with the whole body is aptly illustrated here; the skier can recover less easily if he leans too far in than if he used the comma. However, the inward lean of the whole body makes it easier to weight both skis evenly than when in the comma.*

260. *The Western style; both skiers here are just coming down from their unweighting and are turning toward each other in split rotation, which gives them a square stance.*

Finally, the high bounce, which gets the skis partly out of the snow, also allows the skier to "change edges" by changing his lean to the other side. In effect, the Western-style skier edges by using his whole body, setting the skis on edges by "leaning in."

The Western skier also sits back somewhat, but not much. He is wearing his powder skis—with soft tips. These tend to surface rather than dive. As long as the tips tend to surface, the skier is in no trouble. If the tips dive, of course, he is.

Lastly, the Western skier doesn't wait for the skis to come around to a shallow traverse. He cuts the turn short so that he never gets into a shallow traverse, making a series of long, sweeping christies along the fall line rather than the full parallel turn. This keeps his speed up and prevents the skis from going off across the hill.

What can the Eastern skier do if he is caught in powder with his stiff skis, his predilection for reverse motion, and his tendency to angulate his weight to the outside ski?

He has to follow Western principles as well as he can. He must sit back a bit on the skis; he must unweight more, use split rotation, and a very gentle reverse at the end; he must cut his turns off so that he skis "in the fall line"

261. *The skier here forgot to keep his legs squeezed together. The powder is grabbing his right ski and is about to twist it away from the skier.*

262. *It is possible to use the reverse stance in powder. This skier at Aspen is less reversed than the ordinary nonpowder skier would be at this point, but he is nevertheless in a reverse.*

263. *These two skiers are making wedel turns in powder. Both are about to start turns to their left. The upper skier has already led off with his outside hand to start the split-rotation wedel, or submarine wedel, and the lower skier is about to do the same.*

all the time; he has to adopt a square stance to keep the weight even on the skis, and squeeze his legs together to keep them from being split.

Above all, he ought to maintain good speed. If he can hold his skis together and hold good speed, he has got the powder all but mastered. If he slows down, it starts to master him. This means long sweeping arcs.

It *is* possible to wedel in deep powder; this is the so-called "submarine." It is a split-rotation wedel with very flat skis, and exaggerated reverses. The skier stays very low, and slithers his skis back and forth *under* the snow. The submarine wedel is a forced turn, and it is not easy to force a turn in deep snow. The "submarine" is a series of connected sideslips in powder. The skier *flattens* the skis and *pushes* them out to the side to make his turn, and he *down-unweights* to start each turn. Down-unweighting is the key to short turns in powder.

STEMMING IN POWDER

What of the stem skier in powder?

His best bet is a "step-stem." This means that he should lunge out onto the ski as he stems it. (This is about the only way he can kick the stemmed ski into the turn in deep powder). Then he step-stems the other ski in the other direction. He cuts the turn off fairly soon, so that he stays pretty much in the fall line. His speed will be kept down by the resistance of the snow, and so he doesn't really have to get into a shallow traverse. He must also exaggerate his up-unweighting a bit, which makes the step-stem a sort of leaping stem. The expert version of this, the "dipsy doodle," was invented as a way of getting through powder by the first American racer to win international recognition, Dick Durrance. It is effective, but not aesthetic. The action is reminiscent of Eliza in *Uncle Tom's Cabin,* jumping from ice floe to ice floe ahead of the bloodhounds.

So much for powder.

HEAVY DEEP SNOW

The next condition is wet, heavy new snow, in its worst form called "mashed potatoes." It is a layer of soggy, deep snow of thick consistency lying on top of the base snow. An inch or so merely improves the skiing, but with three or four inches, new tactics are called for; six inches of the heavy stuff is something fierce. The general answer for the parallel skier is to stay *near the fall line,* making "submarine" christies across the fall line on moderate slopes or short, "submarine" wedel turns on the steeper ones. The skier has to keep his skis flat and slicing through this stuff to master it. As with powder, the heavy wet snow makes it hard to turn into the fall line. The skier who cuts his turn short is going to have a much easier time of things. He will constantly down-unweight to start the next turn into the fall line, without coming out of the snow in a big hop. It is better to keep the skis *in* the snow, even when the skis are unweighted, because the critical point of the wet-snow turn is the point where the skier comes down from his unweighting and puts his weight on the skis again. If he comes down too hard with too much edge, the ski will "track" and won't turn.

The skier who is caught in the shallow traverse, or who finds the snow too heavy to "move" at the start of the turn, may then *have* to resort to lifting the skis completely out of the snow to get them turning. In some cases, he will find himself so bogged down that the best way out is to use the two-pole turn. He puts both poles in the snow and comes out of the snow by pulling the skis up under him. He then turns the skis with reverse power and thrusts them down into the snow again, fairly flat and already turning. The use of two poles enables the skier to cut down the violence of his motions so that he has a smooth re-entry into the snow when he comes down on his skis again.

The skier who over-edges in his turn in this kind of snow will find his ski tracking straight

264. *Wedeling in a small amount of powder calls for less of the split-rotation action, but the skis have to be broken into the turn very forcefully. The skiers here are using normal wedel to make their way through powder.*

265. *Powder can be deep: Sepp Froehlich of the Sun Valley ski school making waves through hip-deep powder in a typical powder skier's square stance.*

down the hill. He is now in a very bad position to start the turn going again. In this case, his best bet is to "skate up." He completes the turn with a series of skating steps very much like the Foeger exercises described in the earlier chapters.

STEMMING IN HEAVY SNOW

The stem skier can make his way fairly well through two or three inches of wet snow. For one thing, his speed will be braked by the heavy consistency of the snow. For another, the stem skier turns without any unweighting, so that the problem of re-entry is avoided. But he must not over-edge. The fairly flat ski will shear through heavy snow where the heavily edged ski will stick and start tracking.

When it comes to deeper wet snow, the stem skier has to stay in the fall line and connect the turns. If he gets stuck in a shallow traverse, his best bet is to stop and completely step his tails up the slope a little. Then he is facing downhill and can start off a new turn series.

One final note about deep powder and heavy, wet snow: while ice and boiler plate may be awful stuff, they make safe going (very few skiers suffer injuries in the course of negotiating boiler plate. The skis will slide over it in a fall). Not so in heavy wet snow or deep powder. The skis will tend to lodge in the snow and exert leverage on the skier's legs when he falls. Every ski patrolman expects a fall of heavy stuff to keep him two to three times as busy as on a day when the snow is hard.

It is of utmost importance, therefore, to the skier that he check his release bindings on a day when he is going into deep powder or loose, new snow. (We shall discuss bindings in detail in the following chapter.)

That covers the subject of the heavy stuff. To summarize: First, connect the turns. Second, use down-unweighting in the fall line. Third, keep the skis flat in the snow if possible, that is, don't over-edge. Fourth, use double-pole turns if you get caught and can't start the turn. Fifth, step-turn out if you have trouble finishing the turn. Last, make sure your bindings are adjusted.

Chapter 13

EQUIPMENT I

What to do about spending money for gear and clothes

The question of money is paramount when the skier thinks of equipment. Good equipment costs money and bad equipment costs pleasure.

Possibly the simplest solution at first is to rent one's skis, poles, and boots at a rental shop near home or at the ski area. This is one way out for the new skier. He may decide against the sport after a try, in which case his investment is minimal. But there are pitfalls. The rental shop may be good or it may be bad. Many of them are bad.

The skier's best bet is to rent from a shop near home. This shop knows that the skier is a local person and consequently might serve his needs better than a shop at a ski area. (To be sure, there *are* plenty of good rental shops at ski areas.) The second advantage in renting from a store nearby is that the skier can go in during the week, get fitted, get the binding setting checked (most important!), and get the financial dealings over with—all before he reaches the ski area. This saves him up to 25 per cent of his skiing time, for he is not going to be standing in line all weekend.

The critical feature of rental equipment is the release binding. Most rental places, unfortunately, use cheap release bindings, which is like buying cheap insurance: it doesn't protect you where you need it most.

Second, the rental boot, which is item number two in a skier's equipment priority list, is usually

fairly soft and doesn't fit well. This isn't dangerous, merely uncomfortable.

One way out of the dilemma is to rent a pair of short skis, preferably the two-and-a-half-footer. The short skis don't really need a safety binding, and the stiffness and fit of the boot are not nearly so important on short skis. The skier is introduced to the sport without having to manipulate six- and seven-foot boards on his feet. (Note: the four-foot ski should have a release binding, although this is not critical, and the five-footer *definitely* should have release bindings.)

For about the same money as it might cost to rent a two-and-a-half-footer for a couple of weekends, the skier can *buy* a pair with simple bindings ($12 to $20). He doesn't need to rent poles at all, and so he saves there as well.

It must be noted in all fairness that there are not likely to be more than a small minority of skiers at any area wearing two-and-a-half-footers. If a skier is worried about appearances, it may be that he would rather struggle with the full-length ski—and he might learn faster just through sheer will-to-win. The middle way is to rent a pair of five-footers or buy a pair ($25 and up for wood, around $100 for metal).

Let us assume now that the skier has decided to go skiing at least ten weekends, over a period of two years, often enough to justify an investment in equipment. Figuring that minimum expense for a ski weekend will come to fifteen dollars a day, exclusive of equipment, and, given ten ski weekends, investment in the sport will be $300 for those ten weekends. More likely it will be nearer $500. In light of these considerations, the expense of equipment assumes its proper proportion. It is almost like the old saying about a yacht: if you have to ask what the yacht costs, you can't afford it. If the skier has to worry excessively about investing in equipment, he might not be able to afford to ski regularly. (He *can* afford to sample it, via a weekend or two on rental equipment, however.)

BUYING BINDINGS

The first item to consider is the least glamorous, the bindings. More than 85 per cent of the bindings today are release bindings. The reason is that a well-designed release binding will get the skier out of trouble almost 100 per cent of the time if they are set properly.

Trouble can come when the ski, for some reason, such as a fall, twists or bends the ankle. Even if the skier escapes with nothing more than a scare, the feeling that one's ankle has been twisted hard is a psychological detriment. With a release binding working properly, the binding will let go of the boot before the skier feels too much of a twist.

On a given day, two skiers out of a thousand will have some injury that requires medical attention. This figure could be cut in a half, or better, if release bindings were all properly designed and maintained. Two out of a thousand is not a high figure, but over ten weekends it adds up to two per hundred, or 2 per cent of skiers skiing ten weekends. My motive in mentioning these figures is only to assure you that release bindings are necessary and that, of the people who get hurt, almost 100 per cent asked for it. Either they were skiing out of control or they had bad release bindings, or, as is usually the case, both.

When you buy bindings, ignore all setups that don't have a release at *both* the toe and the

heel. Both are needed. The heel release is usually designed to let go in a forward fall, and the toe in a sidewise fall, although with some bindings both releases are designed to let go in all kinds of falls.

The "unit" bindings, costing twenty-five dollars and up, come with toe and heel together, as a unit. Of these, Cubco and Miller are the best known. Both require boot plates, or metal plates on the boot heel and toe. Both should be shop-mounted, even if you are a good shopman yourself.

The new Gertsch binding is a unit binding requiring no boot plate and is considered one of the best of the current binding designs.

The other kinds of bindings are sold as separate heel and toe releases.

Of these, the new type of heel binding, which does away with the long spring cable that has been a standard feature of bindings for years, is preferable. The long cable has to

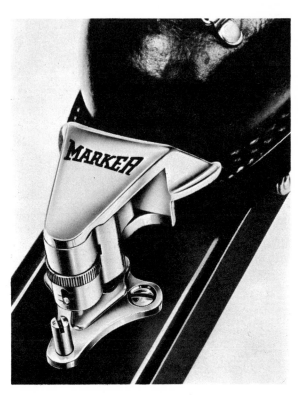

266. *The Marker toe release shown here will, in common with other toe releases, swing the boot out to either side if the pressure of the skier's fall twists the ski hard enough to one side or the other.*

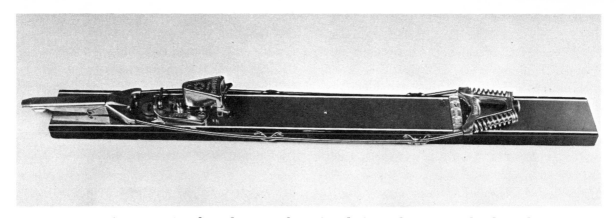

267. *A section of a ski with a toe release (Marker) on the front of the ski, and a heel release (Marker) on the back. This is called the front-throw heel release, because the release is actually made by the lever mechanism at the very front of the section, to the left; this lever is called the front-throw. Cables run back through the side hitches on the side of the ski to the heel-spring farthest to the right.*

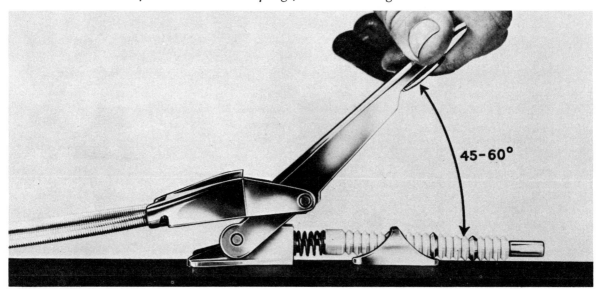

268. *The front-throw release mechanism: the Marker front-throw release, like that of some other front-throws, is designed to flip open, as in the drawing, whenever the pull on the cable gets over a certain tension. This tension can be pre-set. The skier who falls forward over the tips will exert enough tension on the heel cable to activate the release.*

be threaded through cable leads along the sides of the ski, and the cables sometimes stick in these leads and will not release.

The new heel releases are of two types: first, the "step-in" type, more expensive (such as the Look Grand Prix); and the "short-cable" type, which are less expensive. (The Marker Telmat is one example.)

Of the toe releases, the outstanding one at present is the Look Nevada. It gives way under continuous pressures and yet holds you on the ski during short, sharp twists in which you want the ski to stay on. Perhaps the number-two toe piece is the Marker Toe. It releases under the short, sharp pressures of a fall at good speed. It is not as good as the Nevada in the slow, continuous-pressure falls that the average skier would experience more frequently.

Bindings ordinarily should be mounted by a ski shop, unless you know what you are doing. But the shop itself should have a good reputation with the binding-maker. There are shops that mount some bindings properly, others improperly. The safest way is to write to the binding manufacturer, once you have picked the binding, and ask them to recommend a shop in your area. It is worth a trip to get bindings mounted the way they should be. Otherwise you may be taking a lot of the "release" potential out of the binding.

CHECKING YOUR BINDING

There are a few very practical things you can check to make sure the binding behaves up to its potential.

(1) Make sure that the top of the toe piece doesn't "squeeze" the tip of the boot sole. Your boot should be held in the binding by the forward pressure exerted by the heel binding, not by excessive downward pressure at the toe piece. Too much downward pressure on the boot at the toe may cause a binding to stick. If the boot is being squeezed, you will find an adjustment—if the binding is of a reputable make—enabling you to raise the toe piece. The toe piece should "touch" the top of the boot toe but not squeeze it down.

(2) Once the boots are fitted to the binding in the shop, keep the left boot in the left binding and the right boot in the right binding. Don't switch skis from foot to foot unless you readjust the bindings. Boots might be slightly different in length. (Mark one ski in some way to distinguish it.)

(3) Make sure that, if you have your boot notched to fit the binding, that the notches are of equal depth. Unequal notch depths will cause the boot to release more easily in one direction than the other, and you can never get the binding at its best setting.

(4) Make sure that the boot is centered in the binding when you ski. If the boot is in off-center, it will release hard to one side.

(5) Don't let the nailheads or screwheads protrude from the ski or from the soles of the boots. They will block the release mechanism.

(6) If you are using a cable, keep it at a low tension, so that it doesn't "mash" the boot against the toe piece in front. Too much pressure against the front toe piece will raise the release threshold of the binding. (With too little pressure, of course, the boot won't stay in.)

(7) If you have a long cable, the rear side hitches or leads should not be more than two-thirds of the way back along the boot. If they are farther back than that, they may "kink" the cable and foil release.

(8) Use a leather strap or thong to help support the boot and just to keep the ski from running off if it releases (this is a very good thing to have—you may lose the ski otherwise); attach it to the cable *back* of the rear side hitches, not in front, otherwise you may foul up the cable release.

(9) You can lubricate the working parts of your release bindings with graphite to make sure they don't stick.

(10) Check the settings of the release bindings frequently.

A little more detail on this last point: There is a way to check the toe release, roughly. That is to buckle a boot onto one ski and then try to push the empty boot out with the thumbs of both hands. This test should determine whether you have sufficient pressure to keep you in if you are an intermediate skier. If you are a hard skier and need more pressure to hold you in, you can set your toe piece.

There is a much more scientific way of doing this. Buy a fifteen-dollar gadget called Release Check, made by a designer named Gordon Lipe. The gadget will give you a reading on your toe release that will be much more accurate and will check the release on both sides. Release Check will teach you a lot about safety and safety bindings.

As for checking the heel release, the proper way is to put one ski on and then simply try to pull your heel up out of the release by main force, pulling slowly forward. You should be able to pull your heel out without resorting to a forward lunge.

No release binding will safely cover all ranges of skill and weight with one setting. For instance, if you are an expert skier, you would probably want to tighten the toe and heel release more than indicated in the test above; You might want your toe binding set so that your thumbs can't cause the boot to swing it out. In that case, you will be eliminating some of the release potential at the low end of the scale. You could not get out of the binding in a "slow-twist" fall, in which the ski slowly twisted around while you fell. On the other hand, the ski would stay on if you wanted to make some twenty-foot jumps and come down hard. You have to make a choice. But, for the beginning and intermediate skier, it is definitely better to stay on the loose side, at least in the beginning. The slow-twist fall is rare for the expert but frequent for the beginner.

I have dwelt on bindings at length, because of their importance and because badly designed bindings and badly set bindings hold skiing back. Not many beginners come back to the sport after an injury. Gordon Lipe has tested various brands of release bindings and has found that most best-selling brands are pretty good releases and that there are dozens of cheap off-brand release bindings that are no good at all.

If someone tells you that boots are the most important item a skier buys, don't believe it. A poor boot won't sprain your ankle.

BUYING BOOTS

In terms of pure comfort, however, the boot is the prime factor in skiing. Also, it is the most important factor in edge control and in governing the direction of the ski. The skier's foot performs hundreds of little reflex actions every run to keep the ski running in the direction the skier wants to point it. If this seems strange, take a pair of cheap rubber ski boots (such as are made in Japan and sell for about six dollars) and try them. You will find that the

ski won't go where you point it. The reason is that the boot doesn't adequately transmit the reflex actions of the foot to the ski. On the other hand, the skier with the rubber boot can edge a ski fairly well.

The deductions from this experiment are that the *most* important function of the boot is steering, not edging, and that the boot should fit very closely over the whole lower foot, particularly at the ball. Thirdly, stiffness of the ankle of the boot, while helpful in edging, is not so important as the close fit at the low part of the foot where the "steering" is done.

Fit is important to comfort, too. If your boot hurts, you won't want to ski. Your feet are very delicately constructed, but they carry great pressures. Overload one area of the foot and the pain becomes excruciating. If bad fit ends in a blister or "bone bruise," your skiing is over for a while.

There is hardly a boot worth wearing that costs less than thirty dollars, and you probably ought to spend forty dollars at a minimum. The boots form the connection between the skis and the body and they should take most of the strain of the job off the feet. The boot has to be rugged, and rugged leather is expensive. So is good workmanship.

269. *Typical lace boot. There is a second lacing for the "inside" boot under the tongue. Skiers who use the lace boot, therefore, have two sets of laces to work on whenever they want to tighten up.*

BUCKLE BOOTS

Some boots lace and other boots buckle. Buckle boots are the coming thing. They have the great advantage that you can buckle them down in cold weather and unbuckle them on the lift to let the blood circulate and warm the feet. This enables you to keep your boots good and tight in cold weather, which is hard to do with lace boots.

Also, the buckle boot can be tightened up in seconds when the boot warms and stretches from the heat of the foot, as happens with any leather. This means you don't have to take time out to relace. In an ordinary lace boot, relacing can take ten to fifteen minutes, several times a day.

On the other hand, the buckle boot costs more, and it has to be chosen very carefully. The buckle boot fits tight: a poorly fitting buckle boot will cause blisters and sore spots very easily.

When buying boots, particularly buckle boots, take your time. Visit at least three stores and try on various brands. Each brand is made over a different last, and, where one boot may not be "right" for your foot, another may be. Some lasts have a high instep, others a low instep. The instep is particularly critical, because you want to be able to put pressure on the top of the instep, back of the ball of the foot, to make sure that the boot is tight at that point; otherwise the "steering" is lost. But if you put pressure on top of the instep and the boot does not fit under the instep, you will have an uncomfortable boot.

The second critical point is at the heel. The boot should be tight enough so that the heel cannot readily be raised off the sole of the boot, even if someone holds the boot heel and you try to pull the heel of your foot upward. However, this is not quite so critical as the first point. If you have a boot that is very snug and tight over the top of the instep and around the ball of the foot, you can accept a little "give" at the heel.

If you have a typical "American foot," narrow-heeled and wide across the ball, or a long, narrow foot, you may be better off getting a made-to-order boot. But sending your foot measurements to a bootmaker (they are nearly all in Europe) is no guarantee of a fit. These made-to-orders frequently come back badly fitting. The only sure ways are either to have it done while you are in Europe so that the fit can be checked or to send a plaster cast of your feet. Any good orthopedic foot doctor and some orthopedic stores will make you a cast.

When you are trying on boots, wear one thin sock and one thick sock on each foot. This is the best combination for the slopes, and you should wear it when being fitted.

The skier must bend forward at the ankle when he skis, to down-unweight and to execute other moves. There is no sense, then, in getting a boot that is too high at the ankle. It will cut into the shin bone when the skier bends forward at the ankles. This is particularly true of stem skiers. Their ankles are bent forward a good deal of the time. In fact, most stem skiers are better off with the top buckle or the top lacings of most types of boot undone.

Unless you are a hard skier, do not buy a hard boot. Buy a medium-stiff boot. Only those skiers who ski a great deal of the time can afford the luxury of breaking in a very stiff boot. It takes time, and you have to do it gradually, shifting to older and more comfortable boots to give your feet a rest.

The skier who doesn't have time for this and who is stuck with a very stiff boot can soak his ski socks in water, put the boots on over the wet socks, and walk around until the socks are dry. This "shapes" the boot; the same thing takes place, but more slowly, when the boot is being broken in gradually. In effect, the skier has bought a too-stiff boot and has to take some of the life out of it to use it at all. It is better to get a not-so-stiff boot to begin with.

Chapter 14

EQUIPMENT II

Skis, poles, and clothes and how they relate to skiing

In the last chapter, we checked out the two vital items, boots and bindings. It may seem odd to say that skis are not so vital, but they aren't. If you come up with a fair pair of skis, they will do you almost as well as a much more expensive pair, at least to begin with.

There are really two main choices when it comes to skis. First, length: short or long? Second, material: wood, metal, or fiber glass?

We have debated the question of length sufficiently. The question of material is a matter of cost. A set of wood skis will perform fairly well, provided you are willing to pay something above twenty-five dollars for them. But they have a tendency to warp over the summer, which means that your skiing will get lopsided: you turn more easily in one direction than in the other. And they lose their "life" or resilience very soon.

Metal skis, which begin somewhere around a hundred dollars (for the cheap ones), will not warp, won't wear out nearly so soon, and can be resurfaced, top and bottom, for less than it costs to buy new. Also, metal skis can be designed to turn more readily than the wood. Beginner's metal skis are designed just that way. The Head Standard and the Hart Standard skis are outstandingly easy to turn. Head and Hart are the two American metal-ski manufacturers. Howard Head is renowned for his great speed in repairing and replacing his skis if either is needed.

Hart sells its skis somewhat less expensively. Each brand has its partisans. (Probably the best buy in metal skis is the Hart off-brand, known as Mercury. It is the same ski as the Hart beginner, but about twenty dollars cheaper.)

Buying a metal ski from a foreign manufacturer involves the risk that the manufacturer won't back up the ski with service if the skier needs repair or replacement. Also, resale price of the ski will depreciate much faster. There is a good used-ski market for Head and Hart skis here if you want to "trade up."

The more expensive Heads and Harts go to about $175 for Head racing skis, and $200 for the Hart Javelin, a prestige ski. The beginner's models, although they turn well and easily, do not track so well as the more expensive "expert" models. On the other hand, the expert models are harder to turn. You can't have it both ways. A beginning skier is much better off with the beginner's models.

FIBER-GLASS SKIS

The last material choice is among the fiber-glass skis. These are made of everything from 100 per cent fiber glass to a 10 per cent fiber-glass covering on wood skis. Good fiber-glass skis are being made, and the best are very smooth-skiing products, easy over the bumps

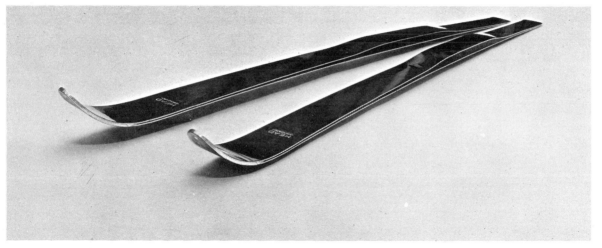

270. *A pair of Head skis. The tip or "shovel" of the metal ski can be made softer, and the body of the ski stiffer relatively to the tip, than can a wood ski. The metal ski does not lose its shape through the years.*

and steady in tracking. But there hasn't been a "shakedown" in the field yet, and many new brands are untested. The longest-standing brand is Kneissl's series—White Star, Red Star. The White Star comes in at about $200 and the others somewhat less. Eventually we will see some good, less expensive fiber-glass skis. Yamaha is a leading economy fiber-glass ski (eighty dollars or so). At present, however, fiber-glass skis are usually more expensive than metal; nor are they—so far—as durable, and they do not keep their looks. (Fiber-glass skis scuff up more easily.) The skier who buys today's fiber glass is buying a ride, not durability.

Of the expensive wood skis, the Kaestle and Kneissl are the best known and are still used for slalom racing by expert skiers, who like the "spring" of the wood ski. But the ski loses this spring, and its best skiing qualities with it, after a year or two of use.

It may be comforting, after all this, to know that the best buy in ski equipment is the poles. Excellent aluminum poles can be had for $12 to $15. There are lovely light aluminum-alloy poles at $25 to $35, but it takes an expert skier to appreciate them. The top "name" brand is Scott who makes an aluminum-alloy pole with a very nice "pistol grip" that helps the skier to flick out his pole for the coming turn.

271. *Howard Head, father of the metal ski. His Head skis still outsell the others on the market. Head spent years working out his design for the ski before he made any money on it. He is now being paid for that labor both in money and in the enjoyment that skiers get out of his skis.*

272. *Hart skis: these run Head a close second in the U.S. metal-ski market. Each ski has its partisans.*

The main question regarding poles is height. I favor a long pole for the recreational skier. Stand the pole on the floor. The handle should come up hard against the underside of the arm, next to the body, when the skier stands normally. The slalom racer may like a shorter pole for maneuverability, but the recreational skier uses the pole for support while standing and while unweighting. If the pole is too short, he'll have to lean over too far to use it. The skier also uses the pole to push himself along the flat and to climb. Here again, length, up to a certain point, is good.

The other pole consideration is the hand strap. The strap should be adjustable—and broad enough so that it won't cut into the hand when the skier leans on it.

The proper position for the hand inside the strap is one in which the skier grasps both strap and pole and lets the strap take the strain, rather than holding the pole handle in a death grip. The skier should be able to use the pole with the fingers unclasped if he is utilizing the strap to take the strain in the proper manner.

WARMTH AND SKIING

The sport of skiing is built up partly of a series of interdependent judgments on equipment and clothes. If the skier starts out with good, functional clothes, the rest of the sport becomes easier. If the skier has warm underclothes, for instance, he won't have to wear markedly heavy sweaters and parkas. He will be freer to move. Also, if the underclothes keep the central part of the body warm, the hands will be warm and the skier will move the poles better. And he will have warmer feet, which means they'll be more sensitive to the proper edge needed for the skis.

The Eastern skier particularly needs warm undergarments. Temperatures in the East can go below zero. If there is a wind, it is impossible to ski comfortably in below-zero weather without quilted underwear. This is rather bulky, soft, pliable stuff, and it doesn't hinder the skier's movements. It is built along the same principles as the quilted parka. A full suit of this underwear costs about ten to twenty-five dollars and can save a weekend. Quilted underwear makes it possible to ride a chairlift at fifteen degrees below zero in a twenty-five-mile-an-hour wind and still be comfortable. (Both BVD and Duofold make quilted underwear.)

The next-warmest kind is net underwear, and after that, double-ply long underwear. Both are useful in temperatures from zero to twenty-five above, but below zero, they are no substitute for the quilted. The ski instructor, who is at the area all week long, has time to become acclimated to the cold and probably does not need anything but net underwear. The recreational skier *does* need it, unless he sleeps outdoors on his back porch all week to get acclimated.

STRETCH PANTS

Stretch pants do make the wearer more attractive (in most cases), and because they are close to the skier's skin, they help him to get the feel of the correct positions more easily. Stretch pants run from twenty-five to sixty-five dollars. The most crucial point about stretch pants is whether the stirrup, which goes under the foot, is broad enough to hold the pants down without cutting the skier's instep. It should be at least two inches wide at the narrowest point and should be made of stretch material like the pants themselves.

The alternative to stretch pants is knickers. They are less expensive and more comfortable. If you are riding a long distance to the slope in ski clothes, they are *much* more comfortable. And they are as acceptable as stretch pants. Levis are acceptable, as well, particularly for those under twenty-five. The levis are open at the bottom, however, and you should expect your socks to get wet if the temperature is above freezing.

With proper underwear, the skier needs only a parka and a sweater. If you have a mountain parka, which is quite bulky and filled with eider down, you won't need more than a medium-weight sweater. Mountain parkas have been coming on the market lately in response to a sensible demand for warmer clothes. Fashion people are so imbued with the idea of "the thin look" that there has been a minor revolt on the part of some skiers. The thin look is great when the sun's out and the temperature stands at twenty-five or so, but below that, it is forbiddingly cool to ski in a "thin-look" outfit.

The mountain-type parka filled with eider down makes sense in another way. The parka is cut to allow plenty of movement, and the skier can wear a light sweater under it. This makes for ease of adjustment; if the parka gets too warm, it can be zipped down. On the other hand, if the skier is cold and has nothing to put on, he is in a bad situation.

273. *Stretch pants. Some models come even tighter and more form fitting. Where else but in a circus or out skiing could you wear something like this? The answer used to be nowhere, but not any more. Housewives now go shopping in stretch pants.*

The cost of the mountain parka is somewhere around fifty dollars.

The standard, padded, insulated, or quilted parka is about half as warm and costs around half as much. On cold days it has to be supplemented by a good thick ski sweater underneath. The thinner, more fashionable "thin-look" parka is also quilted or insulated, but it is not really warm enough, as I have said, for the run of Eastern skiing, although it might fare better under the milder Western conditions or in Europe. The East, by and large, has the coldest recreational alpine conditions in the world.

All parkas ought to have a hood for riding the chair lift. No amount of warm clothing replaces the wind-breaking action of the hood on a parka.

Standard wear under the sweater is a turtle-neck T shirt, and standard headgear is a knitted hat or headband.

MITTENS AND GLOVES

The remaining item of importance is mittens or gloves.

Some wear mittens and some wear gloves. Gloves enable you to handle the poles better, and to work on the bindings without taking the gloves off. But to wear gloves below twenty above, you either have to be well acclimated or wear very warm clothing to keep the circulation going in the hands. The average skier should have a good pair of leather mitten covers and wool liners for the cold. It is no good to ski with cold hands. It distracts you from concentrating on skiing.

Of the leather mittens available, there are two types, insulated mittens and non-insulated mitten covers. The insulated make more sense. If you have adequately warm clothing, you can wear a well-insulated mitten without any liner or undermitten. The undermitten is needed under a mitten cover at temperatures below zero. The undermitten is made of knit wool. An undermitten plus the leather mitten cover makes the hand a bit cumbersome on the pole handle. It is also clumsy to take off and put on a mitten-cover-undermitten combination. But at zero and below, it is worth it.

The outstanding insulated mitten is the "Sub-zero" brand, made by Weiss. It has a good layer of insulation and a silk lining for extra warmth. The Weiss "Zero" mitten has less insulation and needs an under-mitten below ten above.

There are lighter mitten covers for warm weather. For instance, there are mitten covers made of light poplin. But, even with an under-mitten, these aren't much good under twenty degrees.

It is a good idea to have a pair of gloves around, even if you own mittens. When the temperature goes above freezing, most mittens

274. *Medium-weight quilted parka. About right for the Western slopes. For the East, a skier should get a more heavily quilted parka with more insulation to it.*

get pretty warm. And rather than ski bare-handed, it is advisable to have a pair of gloves on. If you fall, you won't skin your knuckles if you are wearing gloves—and some of the ice patches that lie on the slopes can give the knuckles quite a skinning.

GLASSES AND GOGGLES

Glasses and goggles are standard ski equipment for most skiers. The wind, flying flakes, too much sunlight, fog—all require some help for the eyes.

Goggles fog, even though they protect you from flying flakes better than glasses. Even the best goggles fog. (So do glasses, but they don't fog so easily.) There are a couple of good fog-preventive liquids on the market, and a lot of bad ones. Try to find one that works for you, whether you use glasses or goggles.

Except for extreme conditions, such as high (forty miles per hour) speed and high wind, high-quality dark sunglasses and yellow fog glasses are better than goggles. These "ordinary" glasses give you better peripheral vision, they fog less easily, and they are more easily wiped clean of fog or snow. Only racers really need goggles for windless days; in high wind, almost every skier needs them.

Dark sunglasses should be of high quality. Don't buy cheap sunglasses. Cheap plastic dark glasses don't screen out the ultraviolet, and you get headache and eyestrain. Buy a pair with "optical-grade" plastic lenses sold by opticians. These cost ten dollars or so, but they screen out the rays that should be screened out. Good-grade optical plastic lenses will not shatter, although they will scratch up easily. Better a few scratches than shattered glass near your eyes.

If you wear prescription glasses, you can have the prescription ground into an optical-grade plastic lens. Ordinary flat lenses are better than wrap-arounds, because the wrap-arounds distort peripheral vision and fog up more easily.

The best way to wear glasses is to secure them. Drill a very small hole through each earpiece, and then pass a fishline "leader" through both earpieces. Tie the leader so that you can barely squeeze the glasses over your head; then, even if you make a violent movement, the glasses will not wander very far out of place.

The worst snow condition, as far as vision is concerned, occurs when flakes of wet snow settle on the lenses. The best solution for this is to wear a Bausch and Lomb "sun shield" over the regular glasses. The shield can be pushed up when too much snow gets on it, and you can then continue until the glasses underneath also become covered with snow. This combination gives you twice as long a run before you have to stop and wipe off the shield and glasses.

Yellow glasses are best for gray days and fog.

If you wear prescription glasses for distance vision, have the prescription made in optical-grade plastic, plain glass, so that you can use them for dull-day skiing. They serve just as well on a dull day as yellow glasses.

Don't buy cheap sunglasses; don't ski with nonplastic prescription glasses (they will shatter); don't ski with glasses unless they are tied to a thread looped around your head (you'll lose them in a fall), and don't use goggles unless you ski so fast that you need them, because they are hard to wipe and because they cut down on your peripheral vision.

Chapter 15

SAFETY AND ETIQUETTE

Manners and minding your skiing make a better show

Ski injuries are of a nonpermanent kind, ninety-nine times out of a hundred. Fractures, sprains, and dislocations are the typical serious ski injuries. There are other occupations, such as driving and swimming, where the risk of really permanent injury is much higher.

It is immoral to ski unsafely and unmannerly to ski impolitely. These two ideas shade into each other. The unmannerly skier is also likely to be the immoral skier, the one who skis out of control.

The first concern of the skier should be for the skiers below him. Whether they are skiing or stationary, he has a duty to keep from running into them.

The rule makes sense. A skier should be able to start out onto the trail with the expectation that the skiers coming down the trail will avoid him. Otherwise, the skiers on every trail would have to wait until the last skier on the trail above had stopped before he could take off. This would cause a dangerous jam on every trail.

Therefore, it is the skier coming down the hill who has the duty of avoiding skiers in front of him.

As a matter of keeping the trails clear, assume that the skiers above you will keep clear of you. Don't stand around and wait for every skier on the trail above to come to a standstill. You will jam the trail.

Unfortunately, skiers who are standing tend to be timid about taking off, not realizing that they have the right of way according to the rules of the National Ski Areas Association.

On the other hand, there are too many skiers who don't take seriously the duty of staying clear of skiers below. They feel that they have the right to whizz by and yell "Track!" They don't have that right. I would like to see more skiers get into the act and enforce the "stay clear of the skier below" rule among themselves. Everyone would benefit. As a matter of Ski Patrol policy, I'd like to see the Ski Patrol lift the ticket of every skier who fails to stay clear, or who skis so as to endanger skiers below him. In a season or so, we's see a definite improvement in trail safety, not to mention manners.

There is a companion rule: the skiers who *are* standing still should stand off to the sides of the trail.

Even if the skier is standing in the middle of a trail, however, the oncoming skier has the duty of steering around him. Again, this makes sense, because the skier standing in the middle of the trail may have come out of his release bindings or may be in some other kind of trouble.

SKI UNDER CONTROL

The rules apply particularly to blind corners. No skier has the right to come around a blind corner or over a blind drop-off so fast that he can't avoid someone standing in the trail. Otherwise any injured skier would be at the mercy of skiers coming down behind him. If you ski out of control, you might be the skier who runs into an injured skier. Think about that a bit.

One of the first rules of the National Ski Areas Association is that the skier should ski under control. Skiing under control is skiing with the ability to avoid skiers below.

There is a good little trick used by smart skiers to pass by another skier on a narrow trail without disturbing him. (I find that saying "track" or "on your right" or "on your left" is fine, but only when you are just at the moment of passing. Hollering it from way up the hill is likely to confuse the skier below.) The best way to pass is to get in the track of the skier below, make one or two turns exactly where he does, and then, when he makes the next turn, keep going straight. In this way, the skier gets himself out of the way, and whichever way he turns, you clear him.

When you are on a collision course with another skier, pull up. Theoretically, the skier on your right has the right of way, but it is wise to take the burden of avoiding collision yourself. Don't risk running another skier down just to assert your rights.

Never go launching yourself into the path of an oncoming skier when he is going to have difficulty stopping. That is common sense.

Don't take your skis off and walk up or down a trail, unless you cannot ski it. The correct way to climb a trail or descend is on your skis. Otherwise, you leave little foot holes that can trip up other skiers.

There is a rule similar to the "replace your divots" rule in golf. And that is "pack out your own bathtub." A bathtub is a big body-hole made in soft snow by the fall of a skier. You aren't expected to fill the hole completely, but you should side-step up and down the hole a couple of times so that you smooth off the edges and it becomes a smooth dip rather than a ragged hole.

The most elementary safety rule is to wear a safety strap on your skis. If the skis release, it is up to you to keep the skis with you. A flying ski, running down the hill on its own, is a nasty projectile.

If you see a ski running loose, be sure to set up the cry "Ski! Ski!" It will alert everyone down the hill to a loose ski coming down, so they can get out of its way.

Unless it is moving *very* slowly, don't try to trap anyone's loose ski for him: this is a very dangerous thing to do. The point of a ski, even if it is traveling fairly slowly, will do all kinds of damage to an ankle or shinbone. In the case of a lost ski, you can afford to be callous; the skier who lost the ski is in the wrong. Ninety-nine times out of a hundred, a loose ski simply sails off the trail harmlessly.

COMING TO A STOP

One firm rule, often ignored, is the duty to come to a stop *below* a standing skier. If you come to a stop just above him, you may skid into him. At best, you spray him with snow. At worst, you catch an edge and hit him. You should not put yourself in the position of endangering another. It isn't part of the sport to scare other skiers.

The exception to this rule is the lift line: you usually have to stop above the lift line, since you can't go below it. Stop and *walk* up to the lift line. Don't come to a stop right *at* it. You may catch an edge and fall into the lift line. This rule is probably the most widely ignored rule in skiing. Every day you will find skiers skiing into the lift line. I am amazed at the good humor that usually prevails in the lift line on occasions like this, because it is an avoidable offense.

One of the best ways to keep skiing well is to take plenty of rest stops. Most of all, take a good hour for lunch. This is particularly true on the first day of a weekend or ski week, when you may be full of energy to begin with, and yet become much more tired than you realize. A tired skier does not ski well.

In this connection, avoid taking "one last run." It is a superstition among skiers never to say, "Let's take a last run" (it may become your *last* run for a while). The superstition has a good basis in fact. If you are tired and yet tempted to take just one more run, you are stretching it, and this is when you get hurt.

On a cold morning, if you warm up a bit before you make your first turn, you will have a better first run. The first run, traditionally, is a bad one. The reason is that the skier's muscles and his sense of timing haven't warmed up. The quickest way to warm up is to climb up the trail about twenty feet, side-step or herringbone—fast. This will get your body ready for the run. It also starts you breathing. One of the big faults of skiers is that they stop breathing deeply when the skiing gets tough. Lack of oxygen in itself is a mental and physical depressant; if you've had a scare, or are skiing badly, stop and take about six good, deep breaths.

These suggestions make the sport sound a bit grim, but it is the overcoming of the "scare" and the transforming of such feelings into a sense of satisfaction at a good run that make skiing a completely captivating sport.

THE SKI PATROL

As for injuries, most are self-induced, caused by the injured skier himself. In spite of the impoliteness and even foolhardiness of a small percentage of skiers, the excesses of such skiers mostly hurt themselves, in the long run.

The Ski Patrol is a remarkable outfit, composed partly of amateur Ski Patrolmen who volunteer their time and partly of paid patrolmen who spend all winter at a ski area. (Any given area may have all of one kind or another or a mixture.)

Ski Patrolmen are trained to give first aid on the slope to injured skiers and to get them down to the bottom, where they can be treated further. Most patrolmen are attached to a specific area. There is a National Patrol, whose members in rust-red parkas are eligible to patrol any ski area. (Membership in the National Patrol is an honor conferred for outstanding service in a local patrol.) The trickiest duty of a patrolman is to get an injured skier onto a toboggan and ski down, holding the toboggan handles (sometimes there is a second patrolman behind) while he guides the toboggan to the bottom.

The first thing to do if a skier is hurt is to summon the patrol. If you are observant, you will have spotted the location of the patrol phones on the various trails. Most of the little shacks at the top of the ski lifts have phones that connect to the patrol. All patrols have a "patrol shack" at the bottom of the area, usually a room in the base building, and there is usually a patrolman there, ready to go.

This brings up a point of safety. The skier should have an area map with him when he goes up the lift. When he goes down a trail, he should know what trail he is on, and approximately how far down the trail he is. This precaution makes skiing more fun (what fun is there in skiing a whole succession of trails when you don't know where you've been?), and it can be extremely helpful in an accident. You can tell the patrol just where the accident is.

For another thing, it will keep you off trails that are either too hard for you or too much of a hike from the lift. (Some trails end as much as a half-mile or a mile from any lift.) It will keep you from getting lost, and this *can* happen. A friend of mine spent several hours after dark trying to get out of the woods near New York City because he'd gone off on a dead-end trail.

Most ski-area maps, unfortunately, are poor ones. Ski areas won't spend enough money to make accurate, legible maps. And they refuse to mark the trails adequately. Every trail intersection ought to be marked, but it isn't.

Most trail maps do show where the expert trails are, where the intermediate trails are, and so on. And trails have signs at the top, indicating whether the trail is Easy, Difficult, or Most Difficult.

INJURED SKIERS

If a skier is injured, the first skier on the scene should attempt to stay with him and send the next skier down for help, even if it means waiting a bit. The injured skier may become cold and need whatever clothes can be spared him.

The cardinal rule is "Don't move the injured skier." Assume that something is fractured even if there is only a sprain. Leave the skier's boots on. If an ankle is fractured, the boot will act as a cast. (Ankle sprain and fractures are the most common injuries.) Unshackle the ski from his boots, as he lies, but don't pull the boot into a different position. If something is twisted, leave it twisted unless the skier himself (free of the ski) can arrange his position differently. Try to keep the skier warm, and quiet, and reassure him that help is on the way. The psychological benefit of having someone to talk to is important.

Once you start moving the skier around, you are taking a risk. Only a trained patrolman can decide properly if it is worth taking or not. You can increase the damage considerably if you don't know what you are doing.

Again, to alleviate the grim effect of all this, I must point out that the risk of injury is small if the skier knows something about ski technique and stays within terrain that can be handled by this technique. An outstanding example of *not* doing this would be the beginning stem skiers who insist on going down expert slopes. The stem turn in the hands of a beginning skier simply cannot be shortened enough to make it a safe turn on an expert slope.

If the skier tries to work on his technique and knows what it will do, and if he maintains proper release bindings, he won't have much more chance of injury than walking down the sidewalk in a small town.

Chapter 16

COMPETITIVE SKIING—TOURING

Forms and impact of the alpine racer;
potential for United States' skiing of the
Nordic forms of the sport

Ski-racing is on television these days; we may be coming to a situation where the nonskiing public knows more about the competitive side of the sport than the skiers do. The active skier is likely to be on the slopes on Saturday and Sunday when the ski programs are broadcast. The average skier's reaction to a race is to assume that the racers will be using a trail and closing it for public use, more's the pity.

Things may be changing a bit. The impact of television on the alpine races (slalom, giant slalom, downhill) has made the race committees conscious of the public relations necessary to interest spectators. Televised races now start on time and proceed briskly. Public-address systems inform the spectators of the time and standing of each racer. Occasionally we see an American race (such as the 1966 Nationals at Stowe, Vermont) with some four thousand people lining the course and staying until the race is over. We are a long way from the European situation, where crowds of ten and twenty thousand are normal, but the interest in racing is growing, even among skiers.

The three forms of competition closest to the recreational form are the three "alpine" races—the slalom, giant slalom, and downhill. Slalom is a race set through "gates" made up of slalom poles. The poles are set loosely in the snow, so that if the racer strikes one, he'll knock it aside. The racer's ski must pass to the inside of the pole, even if he knocks it over. Otherwise, he is disqualified. He must also pass through every gate, although he has a choice of entering from either side.

SLALOM GATES

Gates fall into two types: the closed gate, in which both poles of the gate are set in the fall line, one below the other; the open gate, in which the poles are set across the fall line from each other, side by side on the hill. Two closed gates in a row constitute a "hairpin" and three or more constitute a "flush."

One can almost say that wedel was invented in the flush. To negotiate a flush successfully and quickly, the skier must make the short connected reverse-powered turns that we call wedel.

Incidentally, the Germans use this word in two forms: *wedel*, the verb; *Wedeln*, the noun. Properly, it is "wedel" turn and "Austrian wedeln." But the latter phrase trips the American tongue, and most of us say "Austrian wedel."

275. *Slalom. Guy Perillat, one of the greatest racers the history of racing has produced, going through a slalom gate at Stowe: reverse shoulder and angulation show how the recreational style and racing styles have the comma in common.*

276. *Billy Kidd, finishing a long sweeping turn into a giant-slalom gate. Turns are longer, speeds higher than in slalom.*

The word "wedel" is well on the way to becoming a single-form expression in our language, whether verb, noun, or adjective.

Getting back to racing, the point has been made that the wedel was invented by racers. This is true of all our advanced skiing forms. Yesterday's advanced recreational form is today's intermediate form, and what was intermediate yesterday is a beginner turn today. The wedel turn started out as a racing turn, became the trademark of the expert recreational skier, and is now being performed by relative newcomers to the sport as the methods of instruction become more and more efficient.

Therefore, if only because some racing forms eventually come down to the recreational skier, all skiers are in debt to racing.

The other part of racing's gift to skiing is that the racing side of the sport gives skiing the kind of publicity needed to make the sport grow. The sport should continue to grow in numbers. The only way that skiing can survive as a healthy sport is to keep on growing. Some of the more conservative members of the sport have bemoaned the impact of the mass skier, but as they complain they are very likely going down a run that never would have existed but for the "mass skier," off a lift that was built, not because skiing is a grand old sport, but because skiing is expanding.

277. *Leo Lacroix starting into a skating turn during a downhill run. He will put his weight on the inside ski at this point, letting the outside ski drop away.*

GIANT SLALOM

The second form of alpine racing is the giant slalom. Whereas the gates in slalom are usually close-set, with sixty or eighty gates in the course, giant-slalom gates are set farther apart. The turns, rather than being short and sharp, are long and smooth. Slalom is more like skiing a mogul hill in the East, while giant slalom is more like skiing in the wide-open terrain of the West.

In the slalom form, the skier usually "comes in high" on the gates. That is, he tries to skin just the inside or the uphill pole of a gate.

This gives him a margin for error and it also means that he is in a better position when he comes out to attack the next gate. Once you get "low" on one gate, it is hard to make the next gate. On the other hand, the skier on a giant slalom course often has a choice of high or low, since he has more time to pick his course and needs less margin for error.

There is a specific "racing turn" that is not yet incorporated into recreational ski systems, except as an exercise. This turn is a "skating turn." It often makes for a faster route between gates. In the skating turn, the skier simply "goes with" the inside ski as he comes out of the fall line to finish a turn. He puts his weight on it by means of a skating motion. He pushes himself onto that uphill ski. Once the skier is riding the uphill ski entirely, he brings the downhill ski up parallel. Riding the inside ski allows the skier to lunge forward onto it as he comes out of his turn, so that he is "ahead of his skis" rather than behind them. Also, it allows him to get a "higher line" to the next gate.

The skating turn needs a bit more room than the wedel turns. In a flush, the skier uses wedel and seldom skates.

The secret of the good slalom and giant-slalom racer is his ability to predict his path. The best turn between gates is the turn that uses just enough edging all the way through to carve into the gate at the maximum desirable spot. If the skier over-edges early in the turn, he will have to flatten the skis later in the turn to lengthen it out.

A very expert slalom skier usually under-edges early in the turn and jams his edges in to make it through the gate. This gives him a straighter, faster path. In giant slalom, the perfect turn has even edging all the way. This calls for exquisite edge control.

A characteristic of the winning slalom and giant-slalom skier is his ability to get his ski poles into the act. If he can pole himself forward between gates, he is that much faster. Since slalom races are won in tenths and hundredths of seconds, poling is very important. The trick is to pole without upsetting your turns. The smooth skier who is poling all the way down the course and who is still fresh enough to pole hard at the end will be a top finisher.

THE DOWNHILL RACE

The downhill, the third form of alpine racing, is a thing unto itself. With a few exceptions, the great slalom and giant-slalom racers have been only medium-good downhillers, while some of the best downhill racers do not figure in slalom and giant-slalom betting. The younger racers, typically, are best at downhill, make their name there, and then go on to become good slalom runners after losing their touch in downhill.

The great development in the art of downhill racing came around 1960, when the French made great strides in this event, inventing an aerodynamically sound squatting position, which they dubbed l'oeuf or "the egg," so-called because it looked like an egg when seen from the side.

The downhill course is essentially a trail that has been cleared of most of the moguls, and designed for speeds of fifty to seventy miles an hour. A winner often averages better than sixty. The racers try to stay low, in the egg or similar posture, to reduce wind resistance. They "pre-jump" the bumps to keep their skis on the snow, since they have less air resistance that way. Jumping into the air is spectacular but slow.

With the exception of Bill Beck and Bud Werner back in the last decade, the United States has not had any startling successes in downhill. This seems to be the one event that is the province of the French and the Austrians, with an occasional outside European, such as Switzerland's Roger Staub, coming on as a threat.

In general, the trend of the United States abroad has been toward better performance as a team. This has been partly a result of a much more comprehensive program, initiated by Bob Beattie while he was temporary coach of the United States team and further implemented by Beattie when he became the first full-time coach that the United States has ever had.

In the 1964 Olympics, the Americans took the first two medals ever taken by American men in Olympic or world championship competition. (The world championship, or FIS, as it is called, takes place every two years, and when there are Olympic games, the same races serve as both world and Olympic championships.) The Americans were Bill Kidd, second in slalom, and Jim Huega, third. Jean Saubert continued the fairly good record that American women have had in medal-winning by coming in third in the slalom.

278. *The late Bud Werner. For a long time Bud was the only consistent United States threat to the European aces.*

The future of American team racing abroad will in all likelihood depend on the success of Beattie in getting a number of high-quality racing programs going in the United States: six or eight such continuous programs at a minimum, so that a fairly broad base for future teams can be established. The old days are gone, when the United States coach held an honorary position given to an outstanding college coach, who met the team for the first time when they all got on the plane together to go to the races.

The new system includes a full-time coach; races in season in Europe and with European racers in the United States during annual World Cup competitions (started in 1967). The training program for United States racers starts with conditioning training in the fall. The program is designed to bring the national coach and all the best talent in the United States together.

Some old-timers may yearn for the days when American skiers abroad were a rare and sometimes beautiful thing: Bud Werner winning the Holmenkollen downhill (the first American to win a European race), Andy Mead Lawrence coming back with a fistful of medals from Cortina at eighteen—then things were really amateur. But, for better or worse, the United States has entered the international race scene on a firm and continuing basis, and the results will eventually show it.

But Werner deserves special mention. He was the first American to show the Europeans that an American could win anything, anytime He was not consistent, just consistently dangerous. He was killed in an avalanche when he retired from racing, after the 1964 Olympics. But he had proved that you can come out of the United States and compete on the same level as the Austrians and the French. They worried about him whenever he showed up at the starting line.

NORDIC EVENTS

This brings us to the other half of the competitive sport, the "Nordic" events: jumping and cross country, plus a combination of cross-country and target-shoot called biathlon.

Jumping doesn't have much in common with alpine skiing except that the skis are roughly, only roughly, similar. The jumping ski is a longer, broader job with more grooves on the bottom and no steel edges on the corners.

The art of ski jumping consists of making a dive off the platform, or inrun, of the jump. As long as the skier holds a good position in the air, he doesn't have to move very much. Then, he must gracefully accept the shock of the landing, some thirty to one hundred yards down the hill, and stand up through the outrun, so that he collects maximum points.

Historically, the alpine and jumping events—and cross-country, too, for that matter—grew up together, often being combined in one race. There were races in which you climbed to the top of the hill, ran down in a beeline, took off over a jump, dodged some trees in a kind of natural slalom, and came out at the end as an all-around racer, if you finished at all. These events were called by various names: "kneikalom," "hopalom," and "slalom," with only the last-named surviving into modern times as a name.

Twenty years ago, skiers were more all-around performers. It was long considered the best kind of win if you could win a "four-way" meet: the original "ski-meister" concept was that you were the best if you had top total for jumping, cross-country, slalom, and downhill. Today, the specialists have taken over, and today the praises go to the individual-event champs. The one exception is the "Nordic combined," a jump and cross-country taken together, whose winner is a pale survivor of the stalwarts who could do everything.

Jumping today is a measure of the specializing that has taken place. Good jumpers go off the jump hundreds of times in a year's training; years back, fifty or so jumps might be tops for the season. But the jumper today goes farther; the early records talk about 20 yards, and today we talk about 100 yards (about 90 meters); on a few very large hills known as "ski-flying hills"

279. *Jumping. Ansten Samuelstuen exhibiting good form. His forward lean is giving him a good airfoil shape. He would be marked down slightly for the fact that his skis are not exactly parallel. Samuelstuen held the North American jump record for several years.*

(not used for Olympic events), there are skiers who have gone up to 200 meters.

A hill is designed for a certain average length of jump, say 90 meters. The slope of the hill closely follows the line of the skier's trajectory, so that the landing is not too violent. When he jumps the larger hills, his take-off speed is one factor that determines how far the jumper will go. The other is how the jumper "rides the air." He must keep his arms close in to the sides, or dead ahead of him, so as to have minimum air resistance and, at the same time, he must bend forward so that his back is all but horizontal to the skis. This makes the jumper's back into a kind of airfoil and gives him a "lift" down the hill. Half the points scored are for distance and half are for form. Form depends on how closely the skier approximates the ideal airfoil and how quietly he holds that form.

Jumping is a top Scandinavian spectator sport and is a good draw in the Midwest, where

280. *Cross-country. The skier has just kicked off from the left ski and is gliding forward on the right ski. Next, he'll kick off from the gliding ski and the other ski will glide ahead.*

there are lots of spectators of Scandinavian descent. Although we've had some fourth and fifth places, the United States has never taken a world medal in jumping.

281. *Typical mountain touring scenery in Austria.*

CROSS-COUNTRY

The same, only worse, is true of cross-country. Typical American finalists run well back in the longer European cross-country world-class championships. We've had lads capable of doing well, but there has been no sensible consistency in this. The reason seems to be a lack of realization on the part of our coaches that Scandinavia can show them something when it comes to training and technique.

The main cross-country events are 15 kilometers, 30 kilometers, 50 kilometers, and the 5 kilometer dash. One United States mile is about 1.6 kilometers, and so these races are 10 miles, 20 miles, 30 miles, and 3 miles, roughly.

The cross-country skier is the peerless athlete in the eyes of the northern countries of Europe —Russia, Norway, Finland, Sweden, Denmark. Any man among them would rather come in the drained victor in a thirty-mile, three-hour marathon than be a hero of sixty seconds of fast action on a slalom glade.

There is no doubt that the kind of skier who can come up to snuff in the cross-country events has virtues that are rare and uncommonly pleasant. There are no "hot-shot" cross-country runners. They are wiry and usually soft-spoken.

Cross-country skiers use skis that are narrow and small, by comparison with the alpine. The whole outfit—boots, skis, and bindings—weighs less than a pair of alpine *boots;* this makes it easier for the cross-country racer to keep up his speed. The art of waxing cross-country skis is a necessary skill for cross-country skiers. The wax must be of such consistency that it will "grab" the snow when the skier's weight is on the ski, and slide well across the snow when the skier shoves it forward. This may seem impossible, but, because of the structure of snow, it can be done. The wax engages the separate flakes of snow under pressure, but slides over them once the ski has started sliding.

The technique of cross-country racing is in "kicking off" from one ski, sliding the other ahead, getting the weight on that, then kicking off onto the next. It is a series of kickoffs and glides, producing a steady, relatively effortless speed of ten or twelve miles an hour over the flat—about the equivalent of a five-minute mile —for distances of ten miles or more. Going uphill, the cross-country skiers rely on good wax and their arms. They go straight up. Going downhill (there are some pretty steep downhills in a cross-country race, at times), they rely on good balance plus step-turns and skating turns. Cross-country skis have no edges to speak of, and they don't make parallel turns readily.

SKI TOURING

The "civilian" form of cross-country is called "touring." Ski touring is an obsessive sport in Norway. The same, to a lesser degree, is true in Sweden. Britons, Russians, Finns (almost as rabid as Norwegians), and the Alpine countries (in the form of high-mountain touring) all go in quite heavily for ski touring. Of all the ski nations, only the United States and Japan seem to loathe touring. This is too bad, because touring can be one of the pleasantest occupations a skier can have, equal in quality to an occasional rare run in fine powder snow. In touring, you move at a comfortable pace, set to the slowest in the group. You can be continuously companionable as you walk, and you are outdoors in the quiet, away from machinery and crowds and man-made paths. Lots of touring is done over unbroken snow, away from any distraction but nature. There isn't anything more genuinely appreciated by a skier than this kind of atmosphere, if he is a bone-deep skier.

What enables touring to be so popular in Norway and other northern countries is the existence of touring trails for day touring, and of longer trails set with huts or hotels for overnight and week-long touring in the mountains. A skier who can come in at the end of a great day's walk to a nicely lit fire and a good hearty buffet is not going to miss the elbow-bending jostle of an after-ski weekend at a lift area.

Chapter 17

WHERE TO SKI

A rundown on the United States and Canada

Skiing in the United States divides into several different regions. The most populous ski country is in the East, where two-thirds of the skiers live. The East's great ski playground is New England, and next comes the state of New York. There are ski areas farther south: Pennsylvania, New Jersey, and down the banana belt of skiing, the Smokies and Blue Ridge portion of the southern Appalachian chain.

The foremost ski resort in the East is Stowe, Vermont, a "major resort." (A major resort is one that has a number of big lifts, a nearby town and plenty of lodging and after-ski entertainment.) Stowe has been tops in the business longer than any area in the East, and it still holds the number-one position. The expert runs of the area, taken as a whole, are the steepest and most challenging terrain in the East. The skier who negotiates Nose Dive, the National, Lift Line, and the Starr has really put away some skiing. Stowe also has intermediate and beginner sections: the Lord trail leads to a T-bar that supports a complex of easier trails, and there is a separate area, Spruce Peak, with two chairs built for the beginner and the intermediate.

North of Stowe, there is only one large area: Jay Peak. Situated near the Canada border, it

282. *Typical eastern trail skiing at Killington, Vermont.*

has a large new cable-car lift, plus the ski school founded by Walter Foeger.

South of Stowe, in Vermont, there is a threesome: Glen Ellen, Sugarbush, and Mad River, all within a few miles of each other. The combined lifts and runs of the three make this a formidable competitive situation with respect to Stowe. There are lots of after-ski places and lots of lodges, and it is an hour nearer the big cities. Sugarbush has a name for glamour. Mad River's top trails are nearly as exciting as Stowe's. Glen Ellen is an extremely good intermediate mountain. North of this again is Bolton Valley, a big area that has just opened. Acrobat Art Furrer heads the ski school there.

South of this again is the mid-Vermont complex: Killington, Pico Peak, and Okemo. The two latter are smaller: good places to get well away from the crowds. Killington has three separate but connected areas and is set in a valley full of inns and with a good after-ski place, the Wobbly Barn, famous for its rock and roll.

SOUTHERN VERMONT

South again, we have the southern Vermont complex: Bromley, Magic Mountain, Stratton, Mt. Snow, and Haystack, plus a sprinkling of smaller areas that don't quite come up to major

283. *Eastern open slope skiing, at Bromley, Vermont, West Meadow.*

284. *Mt. Snow is a modern open-slope-and-trail layout, with miles and miles of ski running available on the Vermont mountain.*

285. *Rugged Presidential Range rings the ski area at Cannon Mountain, New Hampshire.*

286. *Belleayre, New York, summit overlooks typical Catskill scenery. The area is within a few hours' drive of New York City.*

status. Mt. Snow is a supermarket of skiing, with more trails and more lifts than any area in the East. Stratton has a beautiful base lodge, fewer trails, and a name for sophistication. Bromley is almost as venerable as Stowe, and it has lovely intermediate trails and a very good snow-making setup, which often saves the skiing for its customers. Haystack, the newest and smallest, is a mountain that is set in chalets, as an over-all development of living-skiing. Magic has some good expert trails and is much less crowded than any of the others.

In New York, the giant in the north is Whiteface, near Lake Placid, constantly expanding, with the longest and highest runs in the East. In north and west New York there are a number of very good small areas. Snow Ridge, at Turin, is the best known. South, along the New York Thruway, going up from New York City, are the Catskill areas: Belleayre is the largest, with an excellent beginner area and some good expert pitches; Hunter and Windham run next in size and in accommodations round about. The Catskills, largely, are intermediate terrain at best, but they are near enough to New York City to make it possible to drive up for the day.

Brody and Jiminy Peak, in the northwest corner of Massachusetts, are within reach of New Yorkers for day-skiing and are the largest areas in that state. In Pennsylvania, Camelback is the queen area, with good intermediate trails and a fine base lodge.

NEW HAMPSHIRE

To take the next state east from Vermont, we have Cannon Mountain as the giant in New Hampshire. It has a cable car, lots of T-bar lifts, and some wonderful trails. There are a good many places to stay round about. After-ski drinking places are not so plentiful as in Vermont, but the skiers tend to be more serious, anyway. The nearest area to Cannon of any size is Waterville Valley, designed for inter-

mediates and run by ex-Olympian Tom Corcoran. In the next valley east we have Wildcat, facing Mt. Washington. Wildcat's gondola-car lift keeps you out of the wind. A bit south is Cranmore, with its Skimobile, the first major lift in the East, and other lifts besides. Cranmore is in North Conway, a lively ski town.

South in New Hampshire, the big areas are Mt. Sunapee, Mt. Whittier (gondola-car lift), and Gunstock, with its ski school run by Mr. and Mrs. Egon Zimmerman. He was a top Austrian star, and she, as Penny Pitou, was our number-one woman Olympic racer a few years back.

In Maine, farthest east, there is only one really big area, Sugarloaf. It has a gondola lift and miles of trails. There are a number of smaller, very pleasant ski areas north and south in the state.

From the west side of the Appalachians to the east side of the Rockies, there is a long

287. *Tom Corcoran, a United States team member and teammate of Bud Werner, finished his career in a blaze of glory by taking a fourth in the 1960 Olympic slalom at Squaw Valley. He is now putting finishing touches to his ski area, Waterville Valley, New Hampshire.*

288. *The only above-timberline lift skiing in the East is to be had off the gondola lift at Sugarloaf, Maine.*

289. *Sun Valley's Mt. Baldy lies high over the town of Ketchum (extreme right), just down the road from the village of Sun Valley. The area has a name as the most plush in the United States.*

290. *Junior Bounous skiing the powder on Sugar Bowl's Mount Lincoln.*

291. *The lodge, Mammoth Inn, at Mammoth Mountain, California.*

stretch of north country with lots of small hills and small ski areas. But there are a few good middle-sized areas as well, although nothing to excite the expert skier. The best known of the midwest resorts is Boyne Mountain, Michigan. Boyne has a modest elevation, but lots of expensive lodging and chic people. It also has ex-Olympian Othmar Schneider as ski-school head.

THE ROCKIES

The Rockies are the real goal of avid skiers in the United States. The fabled Aspen, Colorado, is the four-star resort with nearby Vail rating three. Aspen has three great mountains, full of steeps, pitches, and variations, while the town of Aspen has the finest display of after-ski that the country affords. It is the skier's City of Lights. There are really four areas at Aspen: the beginner-intermediate Buttermilk; the new development at Snowmass, which is in wooded, glade-type country, with intermediate grades; and Aspen Highlands, with expert terrain, besides the main, renowned mountain, Ajax. Its trails, such as Ruthie's Run, Copper Bowl, Gentleman's Ridge, and Spar Gulch, are hard to duplicate. Vail also has a couple of unique bowls that provide superb powder skiing on the far side of its development.

Vail is newer and swanker and quieter. It has a smaller village and the mountain is great, but slightly less expert than Aspen's. Vail is built on rolling hills.

But, for the ultimate in powder, the skier usually will do somewhat better in the Wasatch Range outside Salt Lake City. This is the best powder in the ski world—Europe or the United States. The reason is that the weather is dry. (Moisture in the air makes powder snow into nonpowder.) The areas clustered outside Salt Lake—Alta, Brighton, Solitude, Treasure, Snow Park, and Timp Haven—have dry, deep snow. The top resort is Alta. The runs here are more extensive and more expert. Alta has just begun to develop its potential terrain, as well, even though it has been in the business a long time.

Getting back to Colorado, there are a number of two-star areas that spot the state. Many have great skiing and many interesting features. Arapahoe Basin, the highest Colorado area, at thirteen thousand feet, has spring skiing way into May and very often glorious spring weather.

Winter Park, Loveland, and Berthoud share the ridge of the Continental Divide with Arapahoe. The four are within an easy drive of Denver, which makes Denver a fabulous town for those who *have* to work and *like* to ski. Breckenridge, next to Vail, is a smaller area with people who like the small-town atmosphere. Breckenridge is almost a museum piece in its entirety, preserving some of the architecture and atmosphere of the old West. Mt. Werner, farthest west in the state, is named for Bud Werner, who was born and who learned to race in nearby Steamboat Springs. It is working toward status as a first-rate ski area but at present is quite modest.

Southernmost in the Rockies are the "southwest areas," Red River, Taos, Santa Fe, Sandia Peak, and Sierra Blanca, all in New Mexico. These draw a good many Texas skiers. Taos is big stuff, with great runs, and snow is never a problem. The others are smaller. Sierra Blanca is a lone white tower and the closest to Texas; consequently it has all been "Texan-ified." Both Sandia (which is right inside the city limits of Albuquerque) and Sierra Blanca have cable-car lifts.

Just north of Colorado is Wyoming, with one vast area being built and expanding yearly: Jackson Hole. This is in the Tetons, and has the most spectacular scenery in the United States. Jackson will be the biggest area in the country when it is finished. It has the biggest total drop and the longest trails.

The other "name" area in the Rockies is Sun Valley. It is the oldest of the western areas, having been founded at one glittering swoop by Union Pacific, and has maintained its prestige as the most exclusive resort in the nation. It is set in the middle of the southern part of Idaho and has its own "village" distinct from the nearby town of Ketchum. There are swank rates and moderate rates at Sun Valley. The Janss brothers, resort specialists and developers of Snowmass, have recently taken over Sun Valley; its lift system is being expanded and an extensive home-building development is planned. Sun Valley's famous Exhibition trail, its great powder bowls, its wonderful Warm Springs run, are enough reason to consider this and Aspen as the Big Two in the West.

North of Sun Valley again, on the Canadian border, we have Big Mountain in Montana, noted for the great steep run down its main face and its late snow. Big Mountain ranks with Arapahoe as a spring ski resort.

THE NORTHWEST

To get equivalent spring skiing, you would have to go to the West Coast, over to Mt. Baker, possibly the only true all-year lift development in the United States. (The snow gets a bit dirty in late July, but there's new snow a-comin'.) Seattle is ringed by a series of big and very busy ski areas: Stevens Pass, Crystal Mountain, White Pass, and Snoqualmie. The ski-school operations tend to be very large here, and there are more people learning to ski per square mile of snow around Seattle than anywhere in the country. As a ski city, Seattle ranks with Denver.

A bit farther south, in Oregon, is a second volcanic cone (Mt. Baker is a volcanic peak), Mt. Hood. Like Baker, it rears into the air far above its neighbors. Mt. Hood is the site of a summer racing camp, and it, too, can run year round if the skiers come. The showpiece of Mt. Hood is the Timberline lodge, a great, ornate, grandiose structure built during the 1930s when the government was sponsoring projects for local artisans and artists. The lodge is worth the trip up the mountain, even if you don't ski. Hoo-doo Ski Bowl is the other Oregon ski area of note, having two chairs to Mt. Hood's five.

In northern California, there are two rather remote resorts with good skiing: at Lassen Peak and Mt. Shasta. Shasta has one of the most formidable-looking ski bowls in the world and lots of open terrain. Lassen has volcanic steam pits at the bottom of its runs and beautiful scenery.

In central California, we have a cluster of resorts on the Nevada-California border, directly east from San Francisco, an easy drive. The most famous, of course, is Squaw Valley, where the United States held its second winter Olympics in 1960. This has become a fantastically large complex of lifts and trails. The valley itself is full of lodges and homes, and up on the mountain two cable cars and thirteen chair lifts buzz skiers up to this peak and that one.

The next most remowned is a smaller, quieter, and most picturesque place, Sugar Bowl. There are no cars in the village, because all skiers come in from an outside parking lot via a "Magic Carpet" lift that goes into the village. The mountain is known for good expert terrain and good dry snow.

The next resort in line, in terms of fame, is Heavenly Valley, on Lake Tahoe, just east of Squaw Valley. Heavenly is at the south end of Tahoe and has a commanding view of it. The area has five chairs and a gondola lift. It is expanding as fast as Squaw. In time, the two will be on a par with the big European ski "circuses," such as Kitzbuehel and St. Moritz.

South of the mid-state cluster is Mammoth. This is a very high and, during the winter, very dry-snow mountain, competing in quality with Alta. The snow stays to June, too, so that Mammoth has it both ways. Mammoth has five chairs and a gondola going up the great saddle of Mammoth Peak. The lodge at Mammoth is an architectural triumph.

Farthest south in California is a group of smaller resorts serving Los Angeles skiers. The largest is Mt. Baldy, the queen of the San Bernardino resorts, with three chairs and twenty-one hundred feet of vertical drop. The newest is Bear Valley, a glamor resort.

Canada has its resorts too, some of them of top rank.

Just north of New Hampshire and Vermont there is the Quebec City entry in the big time:

Mont Ste. Anne, with a seventy-seven-hundred-foot gondola lift. To the west, north of New York State, is the Montreal cluster: the biggest is Mont Tremblant, with most of the very good expert terrain. About ten smaller resorts are gathered nearby, most of them attached to hotels. The hospitality and the French-Canadian cuisine make the trip north to the Montreal cluster worthwhile, the terrain at Tremblant aside. In western Quebec, above Ottawa, one big resort is Mt. Ste. Marie.

In the Canadian Rockies, near Banff, are three areas, Lake Louise, with its great aerial tram, and Mt. Norquay, with nearby Sunshine. This is going to have a big development in the near future. What it offers now is snow and marvelous scenery, on a par with that near Jackson Hole.

On the Canadian West Coast there are a number of resorts on the considerable heights outside Vancouver. The largest is Mt. Seymour, which looks right down on the city. North a bit is Garibaldi, with one big aerial lift and a few ordinary chairs, but it is a mountain with ambitions of the Olympic sort, having the biggest vertical drops of any developed area on the continent, forty-three hundred feet, just a bit more than Jackson.

This leaves us the banana belt, that surprising swath of resorts in the southern Appalachians for skiers out of Washington, Baltimore, and other cities. None of them except the Homestead, in Virginia, has attracted much national notice, but it is nice that they are all there and waiting for those out of easy reach of the snowier north country.